From The Ashes
I Will Rise

The Personal Prophecy

Marguerite Leathley

chipmunkapublishing
the mental health publisher

Published by
Chipmunkapublishing
PO Box 6872
Brentwood
Essex CM13 1ZT
United Kingdom

http://www.chipmunkapublishing.com

ISBN   978-1-84747-929-7

Chipmunkapublishing gratefully acknowledge the support of Arts Council England.

From the Ashes, I WILL RISE
Written April 2012

Bursting out
Roaring,
Soaring now into the sky,
filled with dreams,
my beauty beams,
never question how or why.
I'll spread my wings
and see what it brings;
hear my voice as Phoenix sings of power and
might,
dazzling others who catch sight of me.
I'll do whatever feels right to me.
I've got talent and I have a plan,
nothing can stop me, nothing can.
I can heal you, I can steal you,
I can make you feel too.
Ideas igniting,
so, so exciting,
Nothing can weather the Phoenix feather,
nothing can hold me,
nothing can tether me down,
nothing can tame.

But then a flame
catches so fast,
snatches me back into the past,
burning, yearning,
crying, I'm dying!
Spiralling down and down
And crashes;
Phoenix breaks and turns to ashes.
People gloat, people walk away,
some people have nothing to say.
They knew Phoenix would meet her end one day.
But I'm gonna shock you because each time I
blunder,
I can do something beyond wonder.
I flew and failed,
it looks like my ship has sailed.
Lost my chances, my romances.
Just embers to see of what you remember of me.
But watch me, and have no surprise,
As from the ashes, I WILL RISE.

My story – in prose

I am the Phoenix, the Indigo heart. More importantly, I am Marguerite Leathley. It took a long time to realize this. I have been a sufferer of depression, bulimia, bipolar, borderline personality disorder and post-traumatic stress disorder, and a drug addict. To a lot of other people I was a crazy bitch, evil, a druggie, a slut. It's amazing how the labels and categories other people place on you become the reality you place upon yourself. I'm going to go over my story briefly. There's so much to know that I won't go into explicit details, but in a judgemental world it's important to know somebody's background to understand them.

I was a happy child, a chubby kid who loved her family. The worst of my problems were being picked on for being fat, by bullies in school and my siblings. My world fell apart after my parents had a particularly fiery divorce and, sadly, the last I can remember of my parents as a couple was the vicious arguments they had. There was a divide in the family: my brother and sister supported my mother, and I chose to go with Dad. I felt protected by Dad as he had always stopped my sister picking on me. My teenage years saw a lot of troubles. I was unpopular at school and my friends would easily turn on me. I was very insecure and troubled, desperate not to be seen as a fat loser. I started self-harming, was diagnosed with depression at age 14 and was put on citalopram. I started smoking weed and eventually taking ecstasy. I became dependant on ecstasy, taking it every day. I tried to fit in with a certain crowd and to do so I tried to put on a 'hard' exterior. I started shoplifting and behaving a very different way to the nice, sweet, loving and very spiritual girl I was. My family relationships became more and more turbulent, and the arguments with my sister frequently turned to violence. I had to move out and live with my best friend. I was diagnosed with depression and put on citalopram by age 16, dabbled in drug dealing, became promiscuous, became increasingly more aggressive and took my first overdose. I had psychotic fits of rages, with the worst memory being when I actually stabbed my sister in the thigh with a kitchen knife. I saw a drug counsellor, a family counsellor, an anger management therapist and a psychiatrist.

Surprisingly, I did well at GCSEs and went to college, but needed to drop out because of my drug issues and depression. I got a job and managed to ditch drugs. However, though I had managed to lose my childhood weight through taking ecstasy, I certainly wasn't letting it come back- I was diagnosed with bulimia at age 17 by a psychiatrist. It was so rewarding, making myself sick: it reduced my anxiety and provided punishment for my sin of eating, and it felt like Baptism. I became very thin and quite ill, having repeated throat infections that even meant hospitalisation a few times because I was so weak and undernourished. I would faint a lot and was able to throw up whenever I felt like it, without sticking my fingers down my throat. Eventually I had no control over when or where I was sick. However, it was the most in control I'd ever felt. I was striving for perfection all the time, exercising and working, and I went back to college which saw me getting 3 As at A-level. I was prescribed fluoxetine. My bulimia calmed down a bit with new found confidence, and my future looked promising. I liked to go clubbing with my friends and would drink heavily, but couldn't handle it and would get hideously drunk. I would sleep around more when I got drunk. One thing that had remained constant was my massive insecurity and I felt really ugly. The boys I slept with were just using me and I had only short-term relationships. It was in a seriously drunken state that I endured my first rape at age 18. It's terrifying how dangerous alcohol can be in terms of how vulnerable it makes you, and it's disturbing how many men will take that opportunity. When I was drunk I was taken advantage of many times over the years, the worst memory to date was coming round and being told that several guys had 'had their way' with me when I was out of it. I never reported any of them. In my eyes, I was a slut. I deserved them.

The first year of university at Birmingham was a relatively successful year, I made student friends and went to student parties and performed relatively well in my studies. My weight slipped back on from the 'student' lifestyle, and I was thrown back into being obsessed by it and became bulimic again. In the second year of university, I had several part-time jobs with the course, and this meant a job in a pub. I met local Brummies and was dating a guy. I slowly prioritised my social life more than my studies and my job. My behaviour became more erratic with staying out all the time, insomnia, not bothering going to my course, throwing impromptu parties and chasing after my 'boyfriend' – who I loved, but who clearly did not love me back. My university friends started off worried about me, but eventually started hating me.

I would have massive episodes of hyperactivity and partying, then massive depressive episodes and they could not cope with it, as I could not cope with it. The depressive episodes would mean misery and inability to get out of bed. This was the time of my life where I believe I started being really mentally ill, as I no longer felt I knew what I was doing and I hurt a lot of people that cared about me. I lost all my university friends (I eventually had to leave the course), then my job, then my boyfriend chucked me aside, although it was not the last I saw of him. It seemed I'd lost all control over everything and I was once again suicidal.

I returned to University and this time made a whole new crowd of friends; they were indie rock type partiers and my social life became very exciting, I was out every night meeting new people, men, and becoming less involved with reality and my studies. I started taking drugs again, beginning with ketamine, returning to ecstasy and then I developed a pretty expensive cocaine habit. It was all part of the social scene, a way of life. It felt glamorous and cosmopolitan, and to be part of such an exciting and massive social legacy was amazing. To have that many friends, to be out every night, to be in love with someone, was all I ever wanted to do. Sadly the only thing that remained consistent was the 'out every night' part. My highs were extreme and radiant, I was funny, popular, bouncing with energy, attracted many people to me. The man I was in love with was so unpredictable, and it made me feel massively confused and insecure. I was unable to maintain anything fixed or stable with anyone, because there was a depressive side of me so dark and so bitter that it meant that I couldn't. Sometimes you walk down the certain paths, meet certain people, do things out of complete normal character, and can be in the wrong place at the wrong time. Sometimes there's no expecting what happens to you. It was all to the detriment of my university career once again, I was still having these massive spells of mania and depression and I failed university again. Violence started to creep back into my life as I got into fights a fair bit and had my nose broken by a man outside a nightclub in Birmingham. 'Mephedrone' appeared on the party scene, and we all fell in love with it. A legal drug that felt incredible, our partying was legendary, but thoughtless. I had to return to Wales for a year out of university. I was gutted; I missed everything about Birmingham and all my hedonistic friends. I was all over the place back in Wales, was massively depressed and hated life, and had episodes of rage and self-harm. My parents were really worried about me. I was sent to a doctor and when I explained my history I was diagnosed with Bipolar Disorder Type 1 with psychosis, and put on quetiapine. I managed to get a job on my year out, but used the money to buy mephedrone. It was self-medication more than anything. It helped with my depression initially, but then began to fuel my mania. When I was partying, I would stay awake for three days at a time. I'd be feeling depressed, and have no energy or motivation to do anything and then the mania would strike me like lightning and I'd feel energetic, empowered and unstoppable. This was the same even in the periods I was not taking mephedrone. It was then I started to seek out mephedrone the most. During this period I started going through an ounce of mephedrone over a few days, and, like a lot of people with drug problems I also did a bit of dealing too. It is really utterly terrifying how many young people get roped into doing it to feed their habit, and when I say young, I mean young. I will reveal more later. Drug dealing is not something I am proud of, but I was hardly in the league of the real cunts. I was just a manic mess with a void filled only by intoxicants and psychosis. I was hospitalised quite frequently with the psychosis and pumped full of diazepam. I don't know how I came through that year in one piece, but I made it back to Birmingham and passed the exam to get back into my third year of University. I had stupidly opted to live with a friend of a friend who was not a student and who I knew shared my lust for partying. I guess I always knew that it would mean my life wouldn't settle down, but I felt so different from the students and the student scene that I just couldn't face it. I was bipolar, with a love for three-day binges and I fucking hated the degree. We'd get on like a house on fire.

The house started off with us throwing a few parties and having a bit of fun. It ended as a doss house where loads of people and drug dealers walked in and out without either of us having any control. My mind was disintegrating, more than it ever had before. I had long since stopped taking any medication and was having the most extreme spells of mania and depression that I'd ever had. It's important to note here that I was never really compliant with any medication or therapy, as nothing really seemed to work so I'd always give up on it or just decide I didn't need it. I was losing it completely. I attempted another overdose when my friend started going out with the boy I loved and was sleeping with, and then they created a hate group about me on Facebook. I was so fragile and completely insane, nothing was rational. I started going out with a new man and a so-called 'friend' of mine, who was a drug dealer and a sociopath. He told me he had finished with his other girlfriend, but in fact had not, and when I finished with him he told his own drug dealer, a man higher up the chain and who had been in and out of prison for violent history and had an antisocial personality disorder that I owed him money, and I was told that the house was going to be torched and that everyone in it would be tortured. One of my few remaining real friends had to pay him off for me.

Looking back I will always appreciate the few friends that really stayed loyal to me and protected me. However, it was all a downward spiral that I seemed to wilfully go along with. Despite my 'boyfriend' doing this, and his bitter cruelty towards me, I still went back with him on several occasions, and the unhappiness continued. I was so completely out of that I even let people tattoo me, and one of the drug dealers that came into my house made me get a tattoo on my foot of his name for a small bag of mephedrone. This drug dealer, in particular, loved to bully and humiliate me in my own house. He used to walk in on me having sex with my boyfriend to show his friends this tattoo. He also took my phone when I couldn't pay him back in time. Life was terrifying and I was stepping further and further back into myself. Eventually I lost all the spark I ever had, life was not about parties anymore, but a painful existence, numbed only by drugs. I would show increasingly more disturbing behaviour, but nobody partying in the house around me picked up on, and continued to just trash the house further and further. Eventually, I couldn't go in to university and my life was just a disgusting existence lying in my dirty bedroom, unable to move, speak, or wake up. My mother and sister walked in on this sight, and removed my belongings and me from the house straight away. I will be forever appreciative of this, because I think I was so ill that if I'd stayed in Birmingham I would have died.

When I was home, I stayed in bed for a month, just sleeping. I felt I had lost myself, that any part of me that used to be there was gone. I was agoraphobic and unable to speak at all. It took a while to get back on my feet, but having loving friends and family around me meant that I was able to venture back out again. But my mental illness was not under control; I was still having extreme manic and depressive periods and my mind was still not my own. All the rejections and the fear of my past haunted me, and installed deep in my heart and soul was the broken trust and betrayal many people had showed me in the past I had a complex about who was a real friend and who was an enemy. The final straw was when a drug-dealing ex-professional boxer and violent thug tried to bully and intimidate some friends of mine. He was a symbol of all the horrors I had left behind in Birmingham and I wasn't about to let that evil creep back into my life and touch that of my friends'. He viciously attacked me and it was only because I was able to block a punch to the face that he broke my finger in two places. I called him a 'woman-beater' and then his girlfriend (another professional boxer) attacked me as well. It was only after I had reported this to the police and gone home that it hit me, and I became psychotic and deranged. I felt as though I must have some dark quality within me that attracted all this darkness to me, and I began to feel like I was possessed. Only two weeks later, the violent pair of thugs caught up with me and my friends, trying to get at my best friend's boyfriend. The woman split my lip, meaning I had to have six stitches. Having it stitched up and knowing I would be scarred for life was agony. The facial scar was no comparison to the scars I held inside. I was broken. During the following weeks I was so disassociated from myself I often had black-out episodes where I said truly evil and disgusting things to the very people who'd helped me back on my feet after Birmingham. I had no recollection of them, and when they walked away from me it was heartbreaking, though I couldn't blame them. It was a crippling rejection and I truly believed I was an evil person. I asked my parents for an exorcist. I repeatedly tried to kill myself, and had to see new psychiatrists and have a home treatment team. I was diagnosed with borderline personality disorder and post-traumatic stress disorder.

I was put back on mood stabilisers, anti-anxieties, along with my anti-depressants. I didn't leave the house again for months. Nothing was more powerful than the hatred and self-loathing I instilled deep within myself. My best friend worked in holistic therapy and recommended I see her boss, a Reiki healer. At this point both my parents and I were desperate to try anything.

It was truly the most incredible experience of my life, I instantly felt I could completely trust Dawn, and told her everything. I asked her if I was evil and she told me no, and said I had a great light in me, I was just hurt. The actually act of healing was so physical, I felt a warm, tingling sensation all over and my body actually convulsed. My chakras were being realigned. I saw, before my closed eyes, many colours, morphing and dancing around like a lava lamp. The most significant colour was a purple, many different shades of it, but then a gorgeous indigo, and the colour made the shape of a heart. I heard a voice in my ear tell me I was going to be strong and I saw many visions before my eyes. Many things began to make sense to me. I had a spiritual awakening.

In the following weeks I continued the Reiki therapy, along with my own personal strategy that had become clear to me after the Reiki and that Dawn herself confirmed. It was like waking up from sleep, from a bad dream. I felt like the good, kind, loving person I had not recognised in myself since I was a very young teenager. I started eating healthily, with no further design to poison my body with the shit that it had suffered before; I drank a lot of water and came off prescription drugs. I certainly did not want to touch drugs ever again, particularly the despicable mephedrone. My friends and family were astounded at the change in me. I had been living in hatred for myself for so long. This coupled with a self-destructive force that I was ruled by and a craving for the elusive love, from a lover and from people, had destroyed and distorted my sense of self. I believed I was such a low, worthless person for so long I actually became that person.

The power of belief is incredible. It is certainly belief and faith that saved me, and more specifically my writing. I had always liked poetry and creative writing even as a child, and during the period after I left Birmingham I started writing again. It has been therapy for me, gave me purpose and meant I have been able to record my feelings, my visions and look back over them and analyse them. I will revert back to prose after my poetry. This is a significantly shortened version of my story, but I hope you can understand much more by reading the words that tracked my journey through mental illness in the final year before empowerment.

Marguerite Leathley

MY STORY
Written March 2012

Sometimes I wanna personify my life in such a way
so I can grab hold of it so it doesn't go astray.
Just like a child that's wild running and playing in
the park
Gets lost from its parents and runs into dark.
Don't get me wrong, I had a good family we were
together but for my folks not happily.
Not gonna psychoanalyse every fucking thing, but
there's reasons why there's demons that I bring.
Tried to be seen, tried to fit the crowd, tried to do
anything just to be allowed.
Did everything that meant my folks weren't proud.
My men got what they wanted and then went away,
or if they liked hurting me, they'd often stay.
They were users, abusers and hurt women all they
can.
If I met a nice one I misunderstood and ran.
I went to the city, loved the lights so pretty,
Hung with some people too fucking cool,
I no longer felt like a some sort of fool.
I loved the social scene,
went places I'd never been and saw things I'd
never seen.
I walked down the wrong path, and still can't
believe the aftermath.
I ran 'cause I was hurting, so all those opportunities
deserting.
I ditched my future like it was some trash,
brought all the wrong things with my cash,
ignored my real mates, got myself in states,
gave my love to the wrong types of person and my
situation began to worsen.

Then I became unclean, and I liked being mean.
My life did a complete twist and changed ways,
became a flat-out hedonist and wasted days.
Slowly all that was good and kind and worth a soul
began to unwind down from the sky into a hole.
People walked away from me because the way I
talked was a shame to see.
And I don't really blame them, because I wasn't the
same then.
I beat out with a fist, and went to cut my wrist...
Once or twice...
but I'll try to keep this nice.
The person I was wasn't there anymore;
there was nothing in me that was there before.
I'd either be dancing at my destructive peak,
or more often comatose, unable to speak.
My family came and saw the sight,
and with disbelieving fright they came to take me,
for fear they would forsake me.
It took a while to get anywhere near back to being a
person with soul.
Seemed impossible, an unreachable goal.
I had seen more evil than ever could be told,
but slowly the story begins to unfold,
and I became bolder, with good hands upon my
shoulder.
There is nothing more euphoric than overcoming
your dysmorphic self.
And low and behold I appear to be back to health.
There's been a few setbacks here and there,
but I'd be stupid not to be aware that there always
will be.
That vulnerability is always in me.
I'm gonna try my hardest I say to each family and
friend,

I'm gonna try my hardest to give this story a happy
end.
I want to be something, I want to achieve,
and above all I want you to believe in me.
I've failed you before so I can see why you'd be
concerned.
But the biggest thing I have earned back is my self.
That's more than any prize or any sort of wealth.
I've been given a second go at living,
I'm gonna try for your help and the giving.
I was taken like a child by the hand,
taken from the darkness back to my homeland.
And for this, love you all always, more than you'll
ever understand.

Marguerite Leathley

FOOTPRINT

Unlike a footprint in the snow
a footprint on the heart will never go.
Through winter, summer, autumn, spring
there is never an end to the joy you bring.
Brown leaves fall and frost will weather,
but it cannot move those times together.
Life will change as sure as the seasons;
leave us asking why and looking for reasons.
But when the cold wind finally blows away
you will still be here like you were yesterday.

R.I.P JASON HAWKES

SICK HEART

Now I feel cold in my lover's arms;
our embrace is beautiful, but fragile,
and cold like winter's frost,
for the one I love is now truly lost.
It was not death that separated us,
nor distance nor growth.
Yet I feel bereaved in my luck of choice:
I left because I listened to my inner voice.
My love for him was overwhelming and consuming;
it was a cancer that bound me and destroyed,
A spreading disease that was ugly and reckless.
He did not requite my love.
An illusionist who feigned the beauty of our
passion,
who fanned the embers of my devouring obsession.
But this spreader of malevolent malady,
who bruised my sense to insane,
should be a pitied torturer -
he had known my pain.
Her affection had rearranged him, her flirtation
famished him,
her touch had left him with illness.
I'm sure he was once as innocent…
But she molested him and left the emptiness that
showed me such evil -
or at least they told me so.
I could have taken two turning roads, two paths to
walk, two places to go…
The first was to let him kill me,
to welcome this ill,
to hold myself in harm
and I swear I nearly did…

Because lying in his arms was like all the treasure
of being alive!
Even though it was never real as the kiss of the air
or the whisper of the trees.
I wanted to lay in my destruction always.
But, as you can guess,
the second way I wandered -
I am still lioness!
Still innately have fight
to drag my broken being away from my injurer.
"I would have belonged
for always and longer,
held you, loved you
nursed your weekend self.
But I could not give you health
and I cannot give you mine
we shall untangle the entwined.
Even though I rise from our death bed
I leave a hope for the walking dead.
From your cruelty I'll seek to recover,
but a parting prayer
for my sickened lover."
I journeyed blindly, hurting and
only seeing the past
and my search for survival meant I did last;
but scarred and weak, and famished and empty.
I medicined with other men aplenty…
And now I am held in loving arms
but I cannot see the charms of this life.
I stand in still air.
I listen to silent trees.
I miss him.
And now I know his curse:
"I'm trying to love you,
but I am touched with disease, with cancer caressed,
And now I will hurt you too."

LIFE SCIENCE

Have you ever considered that life is just like a
brain?
And everything is a result of joy and pain?
We are just cells connected in networks of family
and friends,
everything that happens is always means and ends
As things occur in life, and time elapses,
Signals are sent through synapses.
What we do, say or that happens to us is just
electrical stimulation,
voltage changes appearing as some life-event
simulation,
sending signals from and to us by other networks
for greater reason
to the overall system, the power for problem
appeasing
it is action potential, the vibration lives and leaves
to the other synapse which this message receives
alerts for the life change that is due
and sparks another signal
that travels back to you.

I'M NOT SORRY

I'm not sorry.
I'm looking at you and thinking about all you've put
me through.
I'm bitter and wretched and consumed with hate
and this side to me has decided our fate.
I know that because of this personality so comes
the finality of us.
Our friendship is over and all because
I cannot hold my tongue and be the better person,
know right from wrong. I let the situation worsen.
I am sorry,
sorry that I'm cursed to always lose what I hold
dear.
Sorry I've become the person I've always feared.
I'm not sorry
that you are the way you are;
you've pissed me off and taken it too far.
You've lost your temper, lost your mind,
but then so have I. We're two of a kind.
I hate the way you're selfish and will not share,
I hate how much I really do care.
I am sorry
that it seems like I've made you this way;
all I want is the friend I had yesterday.
I'm not sorry
that you acted like a complete prick
and it makes EVERYONE sick.
You're not the only one who sometimes wants to
end it
and what hurts me most... I could not mend it
for you.
I tried, though, I really did.

I am sorry
that I am walking away, from you and everything
that made me smile.
and I know that I have given myself exile.
I am sorry
I could not make up my mind,
make it up in time to find
whether I blame you or myself and what to do.
I am not sorry.
I am sorry.
The best thing to do is to say sorry to you.
I am sorry.
I'm Now Sorry Everything Looks Lost.

I KNOW IT'S RAINING

I know it's raining,
raining in your soul.
I know you feel you've failed your goal.
I know you think that the end is near
and your whole body is gripped with fear.
I know you feel like crying every day,
and if you need to cry, cry away.
I know you feel there's a mountain to climb,
and you are weak,
and hurt from time.
But I can see the hope that you are blind to
and I know that the strength will find you.
All I can say is keep going,
take it day by day,
and I'll be with you every step of the way.

PORTRAIT OF YOU – MY FRIEND

Whenever I write poetry it usually ends up dark
Because did you know that poetry is a glimpse into your
heart?
I write about what rules my mind
life has always been unkind
portraits painted with pastilles of grey
an illustration of what I wanted to say
my words have been as black as they can be
blessings few, don't know what to do
all patterned to see in my poetry.
Then there's you with that torch in the night
a candle flickering with bold little fight
to wash away watercolours that show all my weak
because you are my happy thought above all that is
bleak
I go through the day and smile about you
about how we laugh and how much we can do
only a real friend could make me as happy as I feel
fades away the dark like paint that peels
so it reveals this picture that has a golden hue
it's far from dull
but colourful and wonderful
and the same colour as you.

CUT MY NOSE TO SPITE MY FACE

Have I cut my nose to spite my face?
Departed from some perfect place,
poisoned the wine that we share,
burnt the bread there is to spare?
Maybe I should have held my tongue,
should have watched my words,
stopped smoke infecting the lung.
I've spoken sins like song from birds.
Is it my fault for speaking my mind?
… To prevent myself from seeming blind?
If you act in anger, act in hate,
you'll end up in this broken state.
I've cut my nose to spite my face.
Do not ever act in haste.
Only bitter left to taste.
What an ending, what a waste

L.G.D

Let's get drink,
Let's get drugs,
Let's go mental,
…act like thugs.
Let's snort coke,
Let's bomb speed,
Let's never sleep or ever feed,
Don't be lazy…
Let's get crazy!
Let's get k…icked out,
show 'em the pout!
Let's get laid,
we just got paid,
Leave 'em brokenhearted
finish what we started.
No bed 'til light.
Still high as a kite,
Never let the party end
and then you're a LeGenD.

LUST IN THE LIGHTS OF THE CITY NIGHTS

All the pretty people, what a pretty sight
dancing in darkened places
lights licking sugarcoated faces
hold me close, hold me tight:
will you stay with me tonight?
all the pretty people all together.
maybe we can fill the void
play together, share your toys
play nice, don't be mean.
Music makes me mean,
this ain't heaven, this is the scene
and nothing here is clean.
Pushing past without passion
dual demand is in fashion
free love, cheap love,
just-for-a-moment love.
the city does not sleep…
alone.
In the morning, you'll be alone
but you are so pretty tonight
in this pretty place, it just feels right.
It's not good, it ain't clever.
Pretty people come together.
Come to me, come in heaven.
Let's subtract one from seven.
Hold me close, hold me tight.
We've only ever got tonight.

JOE'S POEM

You brought tears of laughter
and now tears of grief,
God is a giver and also a thief.
Most handsome boy,
you brought so much joy!
BEST of the jesters
all the talents to employ!
Wit sharp as knives,
how you touched lives.
You were so blessed
in all you possessed,
magician musician,
and how you impressed!
How sweet and shy,
guess this is goodbye.
Walk away loved, walk away healed,
into the garden, into the field.
Leave your pain as you go.
I was so gifted to know
the wonderful, the beautiful,
the incredible Joe.
R.I.P JOSEPH CARTWRIGHT

IN CANDLE I CARE

Candle brings smiles across my face
And you know that this is the place for me
When I am with you, dear friend.
Make the daylight over time extend
So companions we can be even longer.
You stood by me and made me stronger.
I will walk with you, my friend,
Accompany you until travelling ends.
But find yourself as we travel,
Slowly the truth starts to unravel.
You are beautiful and lovely and
Sunshine ignites golden sand.
You are that energy, that light and heat
And your good makes my heart replete.
You are the high that accompanies the low
And you have so much of your light to show.
Only endings of joy will reach you now
And if you are wondering how
Light brings more light
Moon is bright because of sun
Light is never only one
Glowing orb does not in mirror absorb
But reflects other rays around
Light travels quicker than sound
Beam lights up surface
And so you will replace the black of night
That you so sadly have to fight.
You will cause joy because of your own good
And it is when this you have understood
Spark will start a sparkling fire
Will be for everyone to admire
Just as I admire you now, dear friend.
So candle, I have love to send.

DOUBLE DIMENSIONS

Daring new Dimensions
Simply as an extension of his own reality
Beginning never leads to finality
Seeing surroundings with eager, eating eyes
Golden grass and tie-dye skies
Whispering up mountains that can move
The other dimension has nothing to prove
In that place he is given the answer
He is a tripper, a traveller, a chancer
Stream travels valleys, dew on grass glistens
Vibrations are another language for him to listen
Beating hearts, music beats his instructions
No normal way to function
No single way, no straightforward junction.
Urban underdog and so very unique
Streetlights look at him as he seeks
Eat the food of dreams and then nothing is as it
seems
Catch him in dark through headlight beams
Never will understand the urban creature
But the main event, the main feature
How can he walk both the roads together?
He walks solo, and smiling into forever.

THE BLACK PANTHER

The theory in my eyes is
the reason behind the lows and high is
Life acts like a lesson to teach us all
With a greater knowledge to reach us all
The Black Panther or what I like to call,
The Bastard-bringer that causes us to fall.

Black and beastly and bound with the woe,
Ripping, ruining, how deadly our foe.
Leaves us weakened like our beings are bleeding,
And panther on our energy feeding
Striding around our unearthly plane
and lives to brings us all hurt and pain
And it seems like this is some great cruel force
that drops us like gravity from climbing our course.
But like all things in nature there is both evil and
good,
and through this consideration I finally understood.
The Black Panther teaches us
how to cope with all the trouble that reaches us.
Beat the Black Panther so you can fight him again
No longer will he overcome, the panther is tame
Turns us into great and powerful beings,
learned of the world and with insight seeing,
And how would I know? I fought the panther now
have this to show.
Remain, strong, fierce and with hope resting on
your back,
And soon you are strong, certain as the panther is
black.

MURDERING LOVE

The murdering love between these two.
Who did not know what to do?
Passion-poisoned young lovers
Could not condition themselves to others
Never felt a feeling
Ever-so mind stealing.
These two loves, how pretty,
Ruining romance began in the city.
He was beautiful but broken inside;
She was obsessed to push sanity aside.
They met and they found a secret treasure,
Was the finding of wealth beyond measure!
I've opened a clam and found a pearl
The joining together of a world
But despite so rich they were homeless in their
passion
Had no home for this, was no normal fashion.
They were mirrored, twinned, matched in a spell
But how sad it was that this repelled
The jealousy was a murdering might
Between kisses and desperate fight.
How they walked hand and hand in the night.
So beautiful, and young and unable to last
How it happened so very fast
The love engorged and forged some pretend
Candle that would burn out in the end.
The desperation they would find
And how it would unhinge the mind.
'I need you, I need you,
I just cannot live if I can't be with you.'
They drank of each others' being,
Blindness stopped them from seeing.
Did not hear how love was weeping

Did not feel how blood was seeping
From growing wound in this vessel.
Bond is breaking, was my heart mistaking?
I will make you cry, make you wish you could die.
How could bond so beautiful be rope that binds me?
How could this sinking love be the one that finds me?
The ship is sinking,
They could not stop thinking
Not one free thought, they knew they ought not to be
anywhere close.
Riveting, rushing, then ruining and remorse.
The embers are running their course.
Like fire burns and then burns out,
Leaves ashes but with love without.
You burned your beautiful selves and I will remember
you.
Why the pain? Why the pain? Why are you making
me insane?
How could one love someone so much to hate them?
To take them up in your arms then break them?
Cuts and bruises on the face,
Limping through a losing race
Passion possessed
Together obsessed
Obsessed over your eyes
Washing away all the wise
Child that shall not share the toy
Just a little girl, just a little boy.
I will remember your candle, your pearl
I will remember the joining world
You were so both so rare, so pretty,
When one love destroyed the other
In the city.

MOON IS YELLOW

Moon is yellow, spirit is strong
Let me show you right for wrong
Moon is bold, moon is man
Moon can do whatever it can
Meddling moon fills my spirit with joy
Musing moon lets my talents employ
Moon is brighter like my futures near
Moon is brave and barrier to fear
Moon is happy, although alone
Moon sits triumphant on its throne
Moon is partnered with the sun
Moon is old and yet so young
I look at the moon and it brings me calm
Moon reaches out with protective arm
To wrap around me, keep me safe
Moonlight smiles on my wanting face
Takes me to its godly place,
Moon is peace, though the world is madness
Moon is friend in all my sadness
Moon is bound to all its power
Bound to in the darkness shower
Glowing orbs
For me to absorb
Let's the worship the moon
Never late, never too soon
The moon tonight will bring me peace
All the worries in my heart release
Moon is captive and yet free
Moon is here for me to see
Moon will forever be
Alone but unmoving
Forever it is proving
It can shine through nights so thick

Moon is bedside to the sick
Moon will always whisper in my ear
Catches the falling drop of tear
Moon will be strange and on the outside
But always holds his face with pride
Moon brings me comfort on so cold this night
Because to me the moon in my sight
Will always be
Maybe just like me.

Marguerite Leathley

WHEN YOU ARE IN LOVE AGAIN

I worry about when I hear you are in love again.
I will lose myself in my pain.
Better to have loved and lost, they say;
I say, I continue to lose in love by day
My heart still hurts in hunger for you
and I know that you have not even a clue,
ignorant that my memory replays all the romance
swept away
like ocean breathes brushes of wave on sandy
beach,
leaves the sand thirsty but unable to reach
back out to sweet, sweeping, serendipity sea
that's how much this means to me.
It's still alive, the thought of how you said I was
amazing,
Each bittersweet bit of memory my eyes glazing
I remember how you kissed me and said there was
no other
And this suffocation still smothers me,
A familiar smell may intoxicate my nostrils, ignites
the air
I don't forget how you smell and it fills me with
despair.
I like to pretend I no longer have these thoughts
When truly it tears me
And then it scares me.
One day my world will drop,
Like when you drop something breakable
It is unmistakable
Something beautiful here dies
No good, but grief in surprise
Will see you saying the same thing and I'm praying
to be blind

Life can be so unkind.
If there is a God, why does he make me hurt like
this?
Why does he make me remember your kiss?
I'll show up with brave face and hope that it will
replace
How much I miss you
And how much I want to kiss you.
In your arms I felt like I could stay forever,
Wishing for that time we'd stay together
My great wound is that I never left your arms
Even after I saw past your petty charms.
How cruel you were when you sent me away
And how I cried nearly every day,
Cried until I was drained of energy and saturated
with grief.
You see you really were a cunning thief
It's probably too cliché
Just to say
You stole my heart like a midnight mugger.
Makes my soul still in its sorrow shudder.
You are an unwanted guest still present in my
everyday life
I got used to it, came to terms with the stinging
strife
But you're still here, inside me
So I still wish you were here beside me.
I loved you, but do not anymore; yet I still love the
way it was.
Hence, I wish when I pray to the very stars,
Why do we love and lose?
Why must I still wear these shoes
That ache my feet?
I walk with you in my every step and breathe you
with every gasp.

My chest tight with wanting you to be in my grasp
You said I was amazing
And now I am gazing
At the stars on clear and clean throw of night
And somehow you are still holding me tight.
But alone, without you, I've lost the fight.
I hope I can finally leave you, the way you left me,
Until then I am waiting.
Waiting,
But not anticipating, because I know you are not
here with me
And I envy that you are free.
I worry about when messenger brings that news.
I will break
I break
Just tell me I was not a mistake.
I walk life with the memory of you.

I PROBABLY MEANT IT

If I told you I loved you, I probably meant it; time passes me by before I've spent it. If I spoke the words, the meaning left as the breath escaped me. If you went along with my madness then you may as well have raped me. I probably hated your company and then missed you, probably longed for you then felt sick when I kissed you. I only wish I could stop and enjoy the pause, just to be my own, if never yours.

THROW ME A ROPE

Maybe I am all you say I am, and I abandoned ship
and swam.
Throw me a rope; it's too much to cope with.
I'm drowning you see - this river is too rapid for me.
I stepped in where it was shallow and was
swallowed by the deep end;
I thought you loved me, thought you were my
friend.
Let me get washed away, let go of those things I
had to say…
Swept, swept, swept away,
all my fears now kept at bay.
I'll go downstream, where things are more like they
seem.
I'll let the current bring me to shore,
I'll set foot on land, the person I was, no more.

ADDICTION

I'll seduce you and, refusing to let you go, I'll reduce
you;
the cracks will always show, but in small ways.
It's what you choose for your days.
You'll get introduced and induced to this by a friend,
a friend that sent you to your end.
You've sold your soul;
you've been swallowed whole by my eager mouth.
My child, my lover, we're both going south.
You'll think you know me, but I'll know you too well,
I'll be sweet like an angel until I take you to hell.
I'll take your mind off your life,
Get in your like a knife.
I'll lie in bed with you at night and tell you that I love
you, but I'm leaving,
you sure you'll keep breathing?
Guess you'll have to chase me, wouldn't wanna
waste me;
you've only just tasted me.
Keep me close, closer than most,
but never tell anyone or ever boast.
You might make others laugh, you'll definitely make
others cry,
you might become extroverted, but eventually shy -
Because you've chosen your life with me and that's
the reason why.
We'll be buried in graves together
or making love in the sky, travelling the road until we
die.
I'm yours now, feel me, just give me a try.

2012

I've always assumed that the world is doomed,
this new year the last;
happens too fast to realise,
too quick to say goodbyes,
the dark overtakes the skies.
Those little lights leave your eyes.
There is so much to know and few are wise to the
way it should be,
what you could be if you just tried -
but you just pass it by, knock gifts aside,
then wonder why.
Maybe the world as we know it will end,
maybe a fresh-born life will descend.
Maybe it's the start of something new,
a chance for me and a chance for you.
In this world we won't be weak and frightened,
but strong and enlightened.
Man won't turn against his brother,
but learn to help and support each other.
So the looming doomsday, this two thousand and
twelve,
may simply be the time to better ourselves.
Maybe I'm crazy to think of either theory.
I could confuse you and be utterly mad.
But I know what I must do... and I am glad.

HELP SOMEONE

When I looked back at my past I only used to glance,
Because there's too many times I missed a chance,
so many ideas that had peaked and died like fleeting romance,
chose to run and hide instead of trying to enhance.
I sought after pleasure and lusted for thrill,
in turn losing what I loved and my soul became ill.
That's not what life is all about.
Look back without fear and diminish all doubt.
If you wanna make good choices forever
be at one with the world and stay together.
You've suffered and been burnt, but have therefore lived and learnt.
Tell this to a friend who weeps on your shoulder and is fearing the end.
Remind them today is hurting and full of sorrow,
but after today, they will walk wise into tomorrow.
Reach out and give a helping hand,
be the one that could understand.
Don't take my advice if you don't want to;
my problems are more plenty than few,
but helping someone else like you,
helping the weak: the best thrill to seek,
is what I'll continue to do.

REAL TALK

I often wish I'd held my tongue.
Would have saved me a lot of strife, 'cause it cuts
you like a knife.
But I like to say what is true to my beliefs, to stand
by my theories,
ask the haters queries:
why they hate on what I believe to be right?
and why all our anger manifests in a fight?
I don't like the violence, but I won't suffer in silence,
and if a thug wants to break me, I'll give what I
take, see.
So if you don't understand this diction, just so you
know it really isn't fiction.
If you can't find sense in this literature, read it in
words that your mind can picture.
If you got something to say, just fucking say it to
me,
'Cause I'm gonna fucking destroy if it's my friends
and family.
I ain't afraid of nothing anymore,
'cause I dealt with all you wrong 'uns before.
You scum, you reprobates, you fucking wastes,
you make me sick, and bitter is what I taste.
You fill me with rage that cannot be stopped;
come at me, then, and you gonna get dropped.
Come at me then, and I'm gonna shank,
this ain't no chatting, this ain't no prank.
But what I'm talking about is what you don't see;
I got more brains than you can bash out of me.
So come at me with all you gotta bring,
and I'm just gonna open up and I'm gonna sing,
I'll speak what's in the dark of my heart,
then watch you slowly get torn apart.

Sticks and stones break ya bones,
knifes and bats cause gravestones;
but words are gonna cut you with much more than
a knife,
Words can utterly fuck up your life.
So come have a go,
if you're gonna have the cheek,
but just so you know, motherfucker's gonna speak!

LIONESS

She runs to battle at my side,
she shows no fear, does not hide.
My lioness beside me at war as always,
we've spent so many days fighting together.
She has been in my battles it seems like forever.
Sometimes it's seemed like we've grown apart,
but the beat of her heart beats together with mine,
the war drums are beating so we know the sign.
I'll go running back to her and wait for her to catch
me falling,
then there will be no stalling as she runs to defend
me
and destroy who seek to end me.
The heroine has love for me that is genuine,
although we've caused each other distress before,
my beautiful lioness will roar revenge to my foes.
Then with all her anger to avenge me she goes.
So loyal to the last of all the fights,
She's there to stand up for my rights.
Lioness makes me laugh, lioness makes me cry,
lioness never even questions why;
if someone's hurt me she does not desert me.
So now I ride into the wretches of war,
lioness is beside me,
just as always and before.

WEARING OUT SHOES

I've travelled many journeys,
worn out many shoes;
it's finding if the shoe fits that gets me confused.
I take those gambles and roll dice that lose me the
game,
leave me unsure who is the one to blame.
I make mistakes; I can't distinguish fakes;
let people have all they can take, then wonder why
my feet ache.
I'll carry on travelling until I know my part,
but every enigma breaks my heart.
I feel prepared for the trouble until it rips me apart.
I give my faith out like flyers on a street side,
and then attempt to make out it didn't hurt my pride
when it's not the real thing.
Each time it's like something just leaves me, I feel
the sting.
I've landed many places, seen many faces, felt
many embraces but to which one lies truth?
Are you really here to the end?
I feel I need proof in case you pretend.
I'm not just talking about lying lovers; it's false
friendship that, when discovered, is what truly
breaks me.
So then on my travels it takes me.
I'll find some new shoes, use them on the journey
on which I now embark.
I've got to keep moving away from the dark.
But sometimes I wonder if I do blunder because the
dark walks beside me or is inside me.

I'll keep travelling in these shoes until my feet
bleed,
I'm going to wear out every shoe until I find what I
need.
I feel I'll run from darkness until the very end,
because I'll never accept that the dark's my only
friend.

TPK

These are the walks and ways of the TPK,
the choices we make don't just last for today.
We have so much fun,
but don't let it come undone;
being in the TPK is saying,
that together forever we're staying,
We gonna party until the end of the night,
just don't let the meaning get out of sight.
TPK means to be friends
even after the party ends.
We might be Trailer Park
but there's no dark
within any of us, so let's start anew for many of us.
A few have gone on their own way.
Just remember that the TPK
is about memories that make you laugh, make you
cry,
TPK until you die
So if you think I'm chatting, that it's some sort of
phase
Know that I'm TPK til the end of my days.
TPK because I love you, TPK because I miss you
TPK because I'll never dismiss you.
Now let's not make days of glory
sound like a sob story.
Let's not be playing if you gnomesaying?
But for god's sake,
please don't flake,
don't flake on The TPK
and your Queen will serve you, every step of the way.

THE LIZARD KING

The king of the lizard
Was, in fact, a wizard
Spoke spells that could change;
The mind rearrange.
People were stranger when you were the ranger
and walked with the living.
Those haunting and daunting words giving.
You broke on through,
Went to the side of the new.
You were not of this earth
and in your death there was rebirth.
The heavens were lit with fire.
You got your desire.
The blue bus did take you,
and did remake you.
Sent you not to the end.
It was never the end.
Blue bus was your real friend.
In the unearthly plane you could never be insane.
Walked into worlds new, with wisdom to bring,
No tragedy, or parody.
Lives long the lizard king.

BREAKING ME DOWN

Be careful what buttons you press,
it causes much more than just stress.
If you're trying to hurt me
you can do that by deserting me, but don't do more
than that.
When I was younger kids called me fat
and, yeh, I was, but it made me believe it was all
that matters,
and soon my esteem was in tatters,
made me control my food intake
and punish myself for making mistakes
in a really sick way.
So watch what you say
It might have made you laugh to make me a joke
but something inside me broke
and it stays the way you break it until something
remakes it.
But rebuilding yourself is not something that is
easily done
so think about outcomes for whom you make fun;
please don't push me, don't tip me over the edge
I have made myself this pledge
that I must be some things and it must be true,
that it can't be all just mean things from you.
So I pledged if it kept on
then I must fix what is wrong.
It must be me.
It must be me.
I pledge to not be.

DON'T SEE THE EVIL, SEE THE GOOD

I should forget you
but I don't want to believe it's true
that I have to walk away from friends like you.
I swore an oath
that not time nor growth
would unbind me from your company
Just please have some empathy
understand like you once claimed to
that I still want to be there like I aimed to
there's something inside of me that takes hold
means that I'll probably be alone growing old.
People ain't gonna stick around
no binds are really bound
no ties are really together
not really, through wind or weather.
But they were for me
so I'm sorry
I said what I said and pushed you away,
meant that I'm by myself today.
Come back to me.
You see, I lack the ability to not make people hate.
Please, it cannot be my fate?
It cannot be.
I've got so much love in me.
You saw it before, before I changed your mind;
leave what changed your mind behind.
In hindsight
I wasn't right,
so let me be your friend again,
I can't let this be the end again!
You told me once, that you understood,
that you get me, and always would;
Please
Please
Don't see the evil, see the good.

HAPPY EVER AFTERS

Happy ever afters do exist
but not for everyone.
Maybe it's time I come to terms
with the fact that life ain't gonna be a fairytale,
no ship's gonna sail to save me from the island.
Snow White was so-called 'cause she was a coke
head:
no prince wanted to rescue her from her come-
down bed.
Beast never met Beauty and with a face so ugly
had to hide,
he had no plastic surgeon so was lonely till he died.
Cinderella had completely normal-sized feet,
so a random bitch, when the slipper fitted, went to
meet the prince:
Cinderella ain't heard from that tosser ever since.
Nobody could climb Rapunzel's hair: they were
extensions and tore out under strain.
Most princesses stay in their towers 'til they go
utterly insane.
Sleeping Beauty was in a coma, so didn't complain.
Nope, life ain't a fairytale; it's what you make it -
you can give it a go if you think you can take it.
Fairy tales might not be real, but you are!
Believe in yourself and you could go far.
Do you believe in fairies? I don't.
But I believe in myself, because most people won't.

BPD

I'm scared I'm gonna lose you,
so that's why I've abused you.
There is no holds barred
because I'm so scarred from what has been
and from what I've seen, been told,
I don't wanna be alone growing old.
Now it all seems to unravel and unfold:
why I fight, fearful yet bold, against anyone that
might be a danger.
I've spent my life loving, then leaving as a stranger.
I create my own family in anybody new,
I drive them to insanity with what I put them
through,
then my worst fear's confirmed and yet could be
predicted.
People are concerned how, with no act restricted,
I lash out and turn into a nightmare;
used to be someone you cared about,
but who could deal with how I scream and shout?
the rage, the temper, the tormenting
saints to distraction, end cementing?
"You're not who you were, there's a change in your
Spectrum of feelings, the great rage from you,
can't have dealings, can't be around you
won't follow, won't surround you
we know who you are now, we've found you.
You are no good to us, so self-involved."
Deep connections diminished and dissolved -
only reflection left to be resolved.
"It wasn't you, it was me.
I needed friends! I needed family!"
Can't control my personality...
impulsive, reckless, so many urges

imaginary power surging
pleasure, pain, purging,
deeper and deeper submerging...
then so much loss, so much regret:
"Come back to me now and please forget,
last thing I wanted was to upset you!
Don't leave me! I won't let you!"
But it was too much, too little, too late,
turned devotion into pure hate.
Self-fulfilling prophesy, obvious fate.
I thought I would lose you, I thought you would
leave
I tried to punish you, to relieve the anxiety
that you would soon say goodbye to me.
Now I've made it happen by trying to avoid;
left a gap, a space, a person devoid
of belonging, of deserving, of worth.
I've buried myself and given birth
to the next chapter, the next time
meet a new acceptance. "This one could be fine..."
but surely it will not, because its end shall be mine.

I'LL PUT PEN TO PAPER

I'll put pen to paper and write. But this time I'll do it with hope in sight. Turn the page away from the pain and rage today. Start a new chapter in the story I'm writing; this dull story that's beginning to get exciting. I think I finally am getting an idea so I'm not gonna think about regretting and fear. It's not usually writer's block that prevents me from this, but this perspective is inventing some bliss, some satisfaction because it's not about interaction with anyone else apart from me, and how I may grow from illness to health. I need to stop worrying about the lost, the losing, the ones who might leave. I need to know and truly believe I can stand on my own two feet. It's me I need to befriend, or even meet. I've needed to get to grips with where my head's at, need to come to terms with me and that's that. Wouldn't even recognise myself if I was looking at my reflection, I've hated myself, been my own worst rejection. I'll put pen to paper and write something new, about a new challenge, something I need to do. Sort out my life, my head, put all those ridiculous thoughts to bed. If I finally start to think about what the shrinks go on about, there's no doubt I could change for the best, so this is less of a story I'm writing, but a test that I'm fighting. Gonna really try now, watch you'll see, gonna write a better description of me. Gonna devote my energy, all my time spending, just to make sure this has a happy ending. I'll put pen to paper and write. Gonna try now, really, with all my might.

SINGLE MUCH?

At the time it feels like everything,
the bird has lost its singing song,
every part of your world is wrong.
But it's only then you feel the bitter loss,
and then later you realise you don't give a toss
It's just at the time you feel like something has broke,
but it's fine 'cause, really, it's a complete joke.
They called it puppy love, needed them, you couldn't
scratch that itch
and then later you realise the only puppy thing is he's a
dog, she's a bitch.
It was a tragedy, the end,
but the years you spend after make you just smile and lay
back.
What was I smoking? It must have been crack.
"I love you and now it's dead. I'm moving away, or living in
a shed.
I'm gonna hide myself away from the opposite sex,
the dick has vexed me. And I can't go on living. Blah blah
blah..."
Pah! Come on mate, who were you kidding?
Wash that man out your hair, no woman no cry, and all
that.
You don't need a relationship to go through life, just go get
a cat.
You don't need a husband or a wife, let yourself go, get fat.
Don't tweet petty tweets on twitter,
be a peacock and don't be bitter.
Be a peacock, be proud, strut on shouting out loud.
Your completely 100% cool by yourself;
fuck relationships they're bad for your health.
Hi, I'm free, independent, here to mingle and I don't need a
man!
Um, can you tell I'm single much?
Probably can.
God dammit, so match.com is the plan. :(

MANIA MUSINGS

Racing, pacing, white rabbit chasing my thoughts
around
listen to that music do you hear that sound?
It's beautiful, a masterpiece...
oh, wait... it's deceased.
If only my brain were a dictaphone
then you could have heard that bass, beat, drone
calling me in to war
"I want to fight, for my right, to party" ...more.
I've got so much love to give, I want to tell you
I just want to tickle you and yell at you.
Fuck me,
I've just worked out the theory of life and the earth,
Man, I've got it... the universe... it's worth
a lot more than just the big bang
what was that song that Ian Brown sang?
My God, you wait, I've got knowledge to give...
fuck me,
it's gone.
My mind's like a sieve.
Bugger. You would been proper on my level, you
get me?
I'll probably have you in stitches if you just let me.
Not actually injuries, don't worry, or maybe I will?
ha JOKES, just having a little thrill
just breaking you down,
because it's funny, I'm a freaking clown.
Mind you, I do have a lot to say
like I love you guys, but that would probably be gay.
Don't sob story the rant.
Let's paint our faces like tribesmen and chant.
Ok now I'm getting a bit trippy,
I'm not on acid mind, I'm just a bit hippy.

Anyway, don't panic,
you've probably guessed that I'm manic.
But I'm having a bloody brilliant time
so I thought I'd do it in complete rhyme.
"No doctor, 'the drugs don't work, they just make you worse'... duuuh??
maybe it's a blessing, not a curse... errrr.
Urmm, what was I saying?"
Feel like galloping, I feel like playing,
I'm a horse that is running through the field,
"Nah, Doctor, honest... I'm healed.
Look, ok, I understand
this is a bit mental... but I feel grand.
Money, I don't need it!
Headlight, I will speed it...
The beast, I will feed it...
Ok, it got a bit dark didn't it?
Might go play in the park for a bit.
Just writing my thoughts down as they come to me
so you can watch them as they run from me
but right now I'm feeling on form, I'm absolutely FINE,
and I've got gifts to bring... "don't you worry about a thing...
'cause every little thing"...urm, line?

FACELESS MAN

My faceless man,
my unknown lover,
been a mystery to me,
something to uncover.
I didn't understand why he wouldn't reveal,
and if he feels or felt what I did.
I can't get my head round why he hid.
It appears for years I've known him
but he has never shown.
My unknown would-be lover,
been trying to discover who you are for ages,
you only let me know bits in stages.
Now I know your name the game ends,
reached the final stage.
I can't dream anymore because I know you're
engaged.
But I did dream,
my faceless man was often the theme.
But good luck,
although I know now who you are.
I wish you well and hope you go far.
My faceless man, my unknown lover,
wish me luck, in finding another.
I've a faceless man, my unknown lover,
known you for years, but it will end in tears.

WOULDN'T CHANGE IT FOR THE WORLD

When it's in the past you only remember the good
parts.
It only lasts if it warmed your heart,
and, yes, it's a good start
to apologise, but more importantly to see it from the
other person's side.
Think of what you went through together, the ride.
You may have cheated, they may have lied,
you might have ignored their calls and they chose
to run and hide!
Break down the walls of the grudge and give
yourself a nudge in the right direction.
Let old views go and let there be a resurrection of
love.
Look above what happened and what was said.
I really hope this one just gets read.
Thank you for shaping me, making me,
or breaking me: you made me this girl.
Wouldn't change it for anything, for the world.

DREAM DEEP

You don't stop holding on to me,
making me smile,
been better than I've been again for a while,
and all because of you guys. Man,
you make me feel like I've got a prize plan,
you make me feel like there's gonna be a surprise
ending,
don't feel like I might have to defend myself again yet.
I've bet on the right horse this time,
I'm running a course and it's turning out fine.
Things are picking up you see and
it's 'cause I got you sticking up for me,
don't need to go picking the place to be,
because you've all got space for me,
time doesn't look like it's wasting me,
or I'm wasting time so I'm gonna walk the line
see where it goes,
got my trust back again and it shows.
Feeling better and I think everyone knows,
my head is high holding,
because you are moulding me into something better
than I am,
not gonna settle for what I can.
I hear a train coming and I wanna jump on,
I wanna emerge cause you're making me strong,
and, yes, this conversion has to be long,
and, yes, I could be regretfully wrong,
but I got a little bit of hope in sight.
Maybe this time I won't have to fight,
maybe tonight I'll get a good night's sleep.
I'm dreaming hard, I'm dreaming deep.

THE DRONE

You can't have a god without the devil; you gotta
know when to chuck the devil out so God can come
over. No one said the devil shouldn't be there, and
everyone knew it would be fun...

The last temptation of man is with us, you realise,
always has been in disguise
but creeping out there as it's seeping everywhere,
invisible except to those who've looked in the face,
been to that place,
gone along with it,
you can escape it if you are strong to it,
it's a panther, a cat,
a feline,
that makes your body a shrine
before it gets possessed.
It's dressed in white
so you can't see its dark nature.
It's full of hate, but it feels like love.
It causes obsession and possession of your action,
and just when you think you know the fraction of
what part of you is still there,
it takes hold of you completely and definitely won't
share.
It smells sweet, it walks on feet of freedom,
empowerment and wealth,
is subtle, sly and delivers in stealth.
It comes from a family of the under boys,
the takers, the monsters, the toy makers,
life ruiners and heart breakers,
who snake their way into your soul
before they take you and drop you in a hole.
But the Antichrist ain't all bad if you can handle

what you've had.
It opens you up and builds ideas; that's how it lures
you and settles your fears.
But as I've mentioned before
its intentions are not to just have, but to test you;
it sees how much fight you will invest into beating it
and how well you can stand when greeting it.
And it's a whole generation that is taking it in,
a whole evolution is what it's gonna bring.
It's gonna cause analysis and then undo the
paralysis of the blocked mind.
In a way the Antichrist is kind:
it's gonna teach us how to be,
once you've beaten it you're gonna be free.
Because once you've looked it in the eyes and
seen its lies and terror,
you won't go wrong, there will be no error.
This year is supposed to bring the end,
and it is the end, because the world is infected
already,
and there's no going slow now, can't steady it.
But the difference is we're gonna be ready for it,
so when you hear it calling,
that growling, hissing drone,
remember when you are falling that you will never
be alone.

DEVELOP. GET WELL. GROW.

Develop yourself, get well and grow,
build on your courage and what you show,
use the last spark within you,
light the fire and continue.
Evolve into what you want to be
and solve the problem of what you are already.
Arise from that metaphorical grave,
surprise everyone and save your own life force.
Endorse your own product and make your tenacity your
being.
Insight causes elasticity in seeing what you are able to
get done.
Look directly into the sun.
It's positive thinking that lifts you from sinking down into
the ground;
surround yourself with positive energy and flow;
remember from the bottom there is only one way to go.
The self always changes and your capabilities are
always ranging.
A wound becomes scar tissue;
therefore that issue makes your skin thick,
builds up resistance to what made you sick.
Show consistency in wanting to better yourself
and show resistance to settling.
It doesn't make you weak if you're the one to step
forward and speak.
If you need help, ask for it in the right places,
work in your own time, but build on the paces
and then feel that sunlight hit all of your faces.
Develop. Get well. Grow.
It is possible, but you MUST know.

STILL THERE

Those of us that know, those that understand,
those that see them walking paths of different lands
and the grains of time never change those that
reached their age,
their hour; some of us have that power to see.
You might not believe me, but I know what will be,
what I saw.
The walkers, some see more of them than others,
it runs in families, in sisters and brothers.
Brain pathways lift the covers.
The seeing, the gifted, the veils that are lifted,
the ones who've worked it out,
descriptors, depicters, know about the dimensions,
extensions,
the non-endings and those spending moments in
between,
hold your breath, sometimes they are seen after
death.
Some people don't believe, and just want to grieve.
Do whatever feels right for you,
but just because they aren't in sight of you.
They will still always care, walking between worlds
and filling the air.
Find strength knowing they are arms-length away in
your despair.
You might not see them, but they are always still
there.

I'M NOT TRYING TO PREACH

I did try, did want you to be, what I could see you are and how far you could reach, and I know I sound like a preacher, but sometimes a teacher is what you need to learn. Just didn't want to watch you fall. But I'm annoying when I call on you to nag you to do what I think is right; it's just I want to fight for your cause, wanted to open the doors that seem closed up. Maybe I should just grow up: people don't wanna accept help when it's needed, so this wake-up call is heeded. Leave them be, because it's meant to be and, one day, they will see.

IS GOD A JOKER?

Is life so fucking confusing because God's finding it
amusing?
Is God just sadistic and artistic in the way he designs this
shit to combine love and the hit, harm, horror, hate,
makes you contemplate your existence, your own birth?
What worth you have in the universe, are you a gift or a
curse?
I'll probably be confused about this 'til they are driving off
my hearse.
Yes, I believe in both theories, if you have any queries
about everything in life, even the strife happening for a
cause,
but that you need to force yourself to keep on course and
win.
I've lived a life of both pure giving, good and then sin.
So I don't reckon it could be karma, because why do good
people get harmed and touched by pain?
Why is God putting such a strain on us - some, I know,
more than others?
Why do cot deaths destroy loving mothers?
Why does crime take away time from victim's life?
And oath-giving husband leaves heartbroken wife?
Why is it that religion only ever leads to war?
Dedication to God means this is what's in store?
Why are the young forced into sex, gangs and guns?
Broken ankle from tackle shackles athlete who runs?
Is God just a sick twat trying to have fun?
Why is the government a complete cunt?
Why are we controlled by looks and social requirements?
Why do old, hard workers die before they taste retirement?

Why do we waste the environment?
How can true love conquer all when, if it's one-sided, then down you will fall?
Why is this planet so fucking small?
Why do we keep it 'just us' rather than all?
I'm sorry if I'm offending you but there is reason in my blasphemy.
There may be no defending this treason, but it is a task for me.
Look, sorry to whine, but I really could go on,
so God please tell me... what am I doing wrong?

RESTRAINED

So now you're giving up on me because I'm not living up to be what you expect. The next step is to take things away; have a good time, enjoy your stay where things are controlled and they have hold on you. Been trying to get hold of myself, but I needed you to stand by me, not lie to me and deny me. Just needed a friend, so this is how it's gonna end. Nobody will listen to what I have to say; each day will never be my own, until I show and have shown that I can conform to your textbook norm, because my actions are like a storm and that's not the form you want me to be. So goodbye to being free, goodbye to what I see, for my own good or not, it's no longer up to me.

LOSING IT OUT LOUD

This confusion is the transfusion of my mood,
the reason why I'm acting rude:
it's because I'm seeing you not being you.
Should I stay, or get away?
You say you want what's best for me, so is this just
a test for me?
See who will rest with me or flee from me,
now they've got what they need from me.
The real ones stick with you,
don't kick you when you're down;
my life has been turned upside and around,
because I don't know when the justice is going to
be seen,
when my slate is gonna be wiped clean,
when this hate is gonna be released from me like a
gate that needs to be undone,
so my trapped mind can be freed and run.
It's not kind to keep me locked inside.
I need to be able to ride out instead of hide out, but
you think I'm gonna let the side down.
So you're gonna surround me, hound me, and
ground me, you've bound me.
All I needed was my friends around me.
I'm crying out, screaming out, dreaming out loud,
but I'm silent, no sound,
no one answers, none can be found.

CATCH ME

So I'd be hypocritical not to be critical of the screams of despair
I've just let everyone share.
I've tried to comfort many with my own past survival
and now the arrival of the black has brought back my revival.
I've seen this beast before and it is one that I have slayed.
I've owed a debt to many and my dues are ones I've paid.
Can't always be strong, you feel the pain; can't always be sane,
so I am wrong on many fronts.
Problem is, my friends, you can't always account for cunts.
Sometimes they mount up, outnumber you,
they rock your reality to rumble you,
so you're gonna relapse, you're gonna stumble too.
Your world might collapse: just be humble and to yourself be true.
You can't always win, you can't always fight,
sometimes you're wrong, sometimes you're right,
but remember morning always follows blinding night.
But right now, guys, in my eyes finding the dawn is not in sight.
Today I'm weak and to slay the beast takes more than might.
I need you to remind me, rewind me to words I have said. So much more -
Help evoke me, because today in hope I am the poor.
I know I've spoken to, awoken you, evoked and provoked the prevention before.
Now I need to know that invention's still in store.
Tell me, please, pain appease, that I will again restore?

VICTIMS OF VIOLENCE – YOU WON'T BEAT ME

Here's for the victims of violence,
the ones who've suffered in silence,
and yes it's a complete cliché to say it,
but for the ones who take it, they don't stop
replaying it.
That's why I'm saying it; because we're the ones
who are paying for it.
You took away a piece of me;
you took away peace from me,
made me scared of going outside.
I've been running and hiding while you've been
striding around with no remorse or regret.
You think you've bet on the winning horse, that
you've managed to take a soul, a strength, a worth
with your fist, your power, your girth and there is no
penalty for your extremity.
You have no brains, you have only hate. You've
caused me pain and made me irate.
You do not care about the fate of the people you
hurt and scar
You think about nothing, only who you are.
You lap up the damage and the destruction,
you're filled with rage ready for eruption,
volcanic vulgarity ready for corruption.
You walk with nothing, but want to destroy;
takes nothing to shake you, the smallest to annoy,
and then you are ready to revenge least needed
cause to avenge.
You get away with everything because people are
afraid
sometimes if it's too obvious they can always be
paid.
You're the lower evil, the thugs, the gangsters,

no real demons, but wannabe pranksters.
You think you hold the power of the almighty on
your back,
so you shower your assaults on those who lack
what you have and what you take.
You crumble them, shatter them and watch them
shake.
You inflict wounds, break bones and split lips.
You feel you have your own law, all at your finger
tips.
You make the good, the meek, feel worthless and
weak.
You don't ever expect anyone to step up and
speak.
You thrive on ruining lives, but have some surprise
when you meet the wise.
You think you've watched them bleed to demise.
You may have bruised me, abused me, and made
me cry.
But you are never gonna make me cover up for you
and lie.
Hey, I'm a victim of abuse, so here's my excuse to
shout its name.
I'm gonna expose you but it sure as hell won't be
fame.
You think you can mash me up, mix me up, maim.
But here's one woman you won't fix up or tame.
You lashed out, I crashed out, but now I'm back.
I'm back with courage and fear is what I lack.
You tried to break me down, take my Queen's
crown.
You really tried to set me to silence, tried to defeat
me,
but I've had your violence and you definitely won't
beat me.

DON'T WAKE ME UP

Please don't wake me up from this dream I'm dreaming,
here the grass is silky and my face lights up with
beaming sun
and I no longer have to run away because I am stronger
in this place today.
The sky forms clouds of different shapes;
this is the land the weak escape to because it makes us
whole.
You may have had a life that once was stolen,
and now you're here and this is home.
So dip your feet in the silvery stream.
Under the surface the fish are a team,
swimming against the current forever,
just like we all do in life together.
But in this place there is only peace,
and whisper of wind breathes your release.
The trees are willow and the soft pillow of earth beneath
them
makes you want to sleep underneath where you are
protected,
veiled in ecstasy by willow's long branch with lucid
leaves.
Everything is here for you, for one who believes.
The world has rejected you
and something has infected you,
but right here lies the cure,
The place for those who did endure and now there is
only rest.
Don't wake me up from this dream, the best I've ever
had.
I don't feel unhappy here, nobody can make me sad.
Don't wake me, don't take me back to the real,
this is the place that I truly feel safe, bathed in light,
don't wake me up now, not tonight.
You can't wake me up now, and this feels right.

THE GAME OF LIVING

Here's me trying to move my little counter forward in
this boardgame of living.
Here's me trying to count my blessings, for having so
much and giving,
and, yes, I've learnt some lessons because there's a
new one every day
and I'll keep spilling these confessions because
there's so much more to say.
There's so much that I've kept under lock and key.
I needed to knock the door to what's in store, and see.
I don't know what the future holds really, but I know
what I hold dear,
what I fear and what I'd like to happen this year.
I'm forever walking on this unstable wave-rocking pier,
squinting out to sea. Sometimes I'm unable to
because there's just too many tears to see through.
I put on my glasses and I still cannot view my
surroundings,
but I feel the world moving around me,
I am blind, bound, but blitzed with sound,
calling me in the direction of my resurrection.
Each knock on this door is deafening and groans,
each foot on deck is threatening and moans under
each step I take,
moaning like pier is gonna break.
Each warning sound stops me and makes me feel
inept.
But I must keep travelling to unravel what is kept.
I'll move my little counter one place forward in this life-
changing game,

I don't know what I might win, money, power or fame.
Or maybe things will just remain the same.
But each time the counter moves, a new life
encounter proves
that life is more than just something you can win or
lose.
Life is something that you can use.
Keep knocking on that door,
try and amount to more,
don't let the waves that break on the peer,
shake you from the path that is clear.
Keep rolling the dice, trying to win.
May not always be nice, just never give in.

THE SUN'S THE BOSS

Today the sun came out and it shone on my day,
nothing to sort out or go wrong today,
and as I feel its breath warm upon my skin,
it's releasing the storm that I keep within.
Don't worry about the bills, the money, the rent,
just make sure today is well spent.
Don't worry about what she said or where they went:
today God has the light for us to rent.
Who cares about the haters saying shit about you?
Don't forget the raters that are getting you through.
Don't worry who you may have offended,
because it can all be mended if you want it to be
or if they deserve it, you see.
People may have stabbed you in the back,
the sun's got rays, but knives it lacks.
You might be jobless, hating work or sacked.
The sun is the boss and that's a fucking fact.
Your past might be full of pain and it seems to rain for
you in every way,
but the sun is shining, it's not raining today.
So come with me, come out, enjoy the sun,
don't know what the day holds, but it's gonna be fun.

JUST UNWIND

Now's the place, now comes time,
things have come together, combined
and things are clearer, refined, come in line.
Think the signs have always been there,
no odds or even, just fair,
relieving the scare,
calming and soothing,
worries are removing
and you're becoming aware.
Do you even give a fuck? Do you even care?
Have we the brain storage to spare
'bout all the things that ain't worthwhile?
Stop running and walk the mile.
Be cunning and sleek in style.
Laugh and the world laughs with you,
cry and you cry alone,
get in the motion, get in the zone.
Have a projection of a happy reflection,
now's the place, now's the time, kick back, just
unwind.

GETTING OFF THE GEAR

You thought it couldn't be,
a reality above the vulgarity of your existence,
and no amount of persistence could get you out of
the grasp of it,
its rasping breath on the back of your neck,
the wreck of your being, and what everyone else
was seeing,
looking down on you, frowning on you,
drowning you in glares
and stabbing you with stares
when you ventured out,
the regret, the fear, the doubt,
in your own self and what people thought of you,
what had been taught to you
and what you ignored.
It wasn't for fun, because you were just bored.
You wanted to feel more, be adored,
above what you could even imagine or think of,
and this is what brought you to the brink of the
edge of hell.
You looked deep into its heart while ecstasy tore
you apart with each swell
and there was no going back to the start.
But you beat the beautiful; you stood up to its
power.
You suffered every second... second, minute, hour.
You endured the greatest of pain,
you were beaten with the cane.
You faced the worst state,
as the chemicals leaving you that had been thieving
you were dragged back to straight.
You made love to the beast then stabbed it in the
chest,

it felt so good, but was the ultimate test.
To keep loving it and laying with it, and then spend
a life time or a death paying for it.
You shivered in its absence as you felt abstinence
for your love.
Before you recovered you discovered how it felt to
have that warm rush whisper, 'hush'
like a lullaby in your ear.
The weeping, the crying, the tears escaping you.
This beast had been raping you.
But you felt every agonizing and antagonizing
withdrawal as you were crawling away from it...
and away you'll stay from it.
Must be like hearing a baby weeping and wanting
to run to it as the drug is seeping out of you.
The junk, the smack, the gear.
You got it out of you and showed no fear.
You didn't let it bring you further down,
you chose life and now you've found your
redemption.
So I think it's worth a mention.
No more heroin, you are genuine in your lust for
living.
You got your second chance now; thank God for
giving it to you.
Fresh start now, something brand new.
Well done, we're proud of you.

PHOBIAS

Sock, alone, without other, on the floor
grips with fear, can't move no more.
Where is its partner? Where is its pair?
Or loose hair, tufts of it fallen from the brush,
gives you that electric rush of pure squeamish
sickness.
There is nothing about this that's ridiculous,
tick, tick, tick, you've clocked the thing that makes
you sick.
Bag is open THAT BAG IS OPEN, someone could
put in fingers
close that bag or this tingle lingers
up and down my spine.
DON'T drink red wine in the living room;
if it spills we'll meet our doom.
Buttons on clothes, bed sheets, or even worse,
a solo button brings you a curse.
Avoid avoid avoid it.
I'm annoyed you let it occur,
can't carry on as you were.
No peepers please, in open closet door,
no gaps please, I can't ignore
the gap in the curtain or the blind
close it please, be most kind.
Baked beans on toast
I fear the most.
Who could eat them? Who would want to be so
vile?
I suffer phobias, have done for a while.
Yes, quite a few are irrational, irrational fears
but the human race has had them for years.
Centuries ago, spiders could kill you, eat you;
that's why you scream when spider meets you.

A snake, a snake, would wrap around you
crush you and break,
so what's stupid about running from the reptile
house?
I'd rather not meet the fate of, say, a mouse.
So maybe every fear and phobia is okay,
because maybe one day
deep, deep into the past, your stupid fear
was rational and crystal clear.
But watch that sock! Alone on the floor!
Look who peeps through cupboard door!
You call it a phobia, an irrational fear,
but I will avoid death in the end, my dear.

SELFISH

Sometimes people are so self absorbed it makes me sick;
look around you or what you want you self-righteous prick
It's like a terrorist attack had just happened
and you ain't noticed- you're too engrossed in the most trivial of shit.
Someone just stabbed your Nan, you wouldn't notice one bit.
Okay, that was a bit mean, bit harsh,
but your brain is like a marsh of yourself,
you're trudging through... thinking about only you
when the grass is greener and the sky is blue.
Every piece of advice is a criticism,
nothing is constructed.
If it goes into debate then something has erupted.
If I do something nice for you,
you proceed to remind me how much you've done for me,
and, yeah, I get you're insecure, but it ain't no fun for me.
I'm not a loan shark, I'm your mate,
if you can't pay me back yet, I can wait,
but I don't need you to bash on about how you've lent me cash.
It's getting fucking irritating, a bit like a rash.
There're people in this world who are in so much pain,
you having the audacity to say you hurt drives me insane
because you don't have the capacity to know what it must be like for them.
You've got everything you need, remember that.

You're driving at speed, but you're driving inside.
Have a little respect, now, have a little pride.
It's not all about you; it's about others, too. Don't
get me wrong,
I know I belong in these verses somewhere before,
but they were curses and I wanted more.
It doesn't do be so self involved;
I feel I have evolved from thinking it's all about me.
That's why I'm writing this, so maybe you'll see.
Check your eyesight, look around, future's bright,
things are sound.
And, yes, I can see sometimes we ALL do it,
gets a bit ME, ME, ME,
but have some respect for those who are truly are
in need.
Unhappy families or no families at all,
barriers blocking, imprisoning walls.
You have feast and they have famine;
so examine yourself, look at your own path,
your luck your opportunity,
be a community not a number oner,
because if you stay like this, your mates will do a
runner.
Now get out of your head, get out of bed
and be thankful for life, for once, instead.

THINK TWICE

Okay, I'll admit, I'm looking for some romance,
but I'm up for a laugh given half the chance.
The lies that guys create to get into pants irritate
me.
People say you should see it coming, but they think
of new ones every day,
think of new creations of something to say.
I like some recreation, I like a little play,
but for God's sake just don't do it that way.
I'm a woman, I got needs, but what's the point
planting seeds?
Just tell me straight you're after a glorified wank;
what's the point in this whole fucking prank?
'Babe, I love you, it's only you, but I'll put a football
above you.'
'Girl, I love you to bits... but see, that girl over there
has mesmerising tits.'
'I swear I'm not cheating on you, (just meeting a
few different girls, and telling them, too, that they're
my world).' And when the shit kicks off you'll watch
as hair gets torn out.
Lads, don't bother, just get the porn out if you want
a fantasy life,
don't actually call each of them your potential wife,
every poor lady.
It's just kind of really fucking shady.
I'm not saying just stick to the one; have fun, get
yourself out there,
just don't rope in the beaver by being a deceiver.
Tell them they're beautiful, tell them they're sweet,
but why lower yourself and repeat this pattern of
making girls meat?
It really beats us ladies down when you don't call,

but hey you're fine, you got laid!
And you're acting like dogs that should get spayed.
Let's be honest, too, lads.
You weren't always bad.
There was probably a girl growing up who showed you up
and broke your little teenage heart.
Maybe you had no luck from the start,
Maybe mum left dad, so that's why women are tarts.
Maybe you follow an alpha male who imparts this wisdom that gash is gash,
now let's get on the lash and try and get some.
Anything just to come.
The lads who are worst sort of pricks usually have the smallest dicks.
Anyway, it's all about neuroscience, it ain't all your fault, a neurotransmitter commits all this shit.
Let's fuck, let's get it on, oxytocin is released and that's where it goes wrong.
Lasts ages for women, but for men not so long,
... so girls, when they are spooning you,
they're really desperate to be tuning into Sky Sports,
and they definitely ain't sharing the same thoughts as you.
See, I did pay attention during my degree, didn't just waste time chasing willy.
They want to get rid of you as soon as they can, and no, it's not the same for every man.
But I've played the game and collected them all,
I like to catch 'em all like with a Pokemon ball.
Try each one for size, and no, not on about their penis, you genius;
it's about trying to see if someone will surprise,

but I'm starting to realise that maybe they are literally all the same.
No, not all guys, but the majority are to blame.
So my frustration means castration for the next guy who lies to my face,
or at least a kick in the balls to put you in your place.
So yeah, you think I'm sexy? You like my brown eyes, so that's why you text me.
Thanks for going to the trouble to tell me I've got blowjob lips -
just let me give you some tips,
Try not to lie to me about your intentions, because you may get a few mentions in the obituary page.
Bit extreme guys, but it's got to that stage!
I'm up for a giggle, but don't wriggle into my mind.
I'm a little bit crazy, you might not like what you find.
I'm loving, funny, original and kind.
But, baby, handsome... I'm not blind.
So facebook me, tweet at me, comment... it's nice.
But you think you can play me, honey, think twice!

CRACK IN THE GLASS

Crack in the glass,
the fragile past is patterned in her face.
But then beauty, power and grace is there also,
although the crack in the glass means she can't, in
the mirror, see
what she is, who she can be.
There were once times of glory.
Don't get me wrong, she's a success story,
but the wars she's dealt with would melt the rest of
us.
You look up from your tears because a hand
appears in comfort on your knee
and you see those jewelled eyes.
You look on the face and relax in your surprise.
You look and see proof in the prize,
the treasure of human capability,
just 'cause there's stability in some things,
some people don't change whatever life brings.
Shit cracked the glass but you're always on task,
you're always there to give no matter what is
asked.
I know you've had a bad reputation,
but then the explanation is your sparkle
and there's loads of magpies.
But those jewelled eyes are the deliverance of your
soul,
something you use to help, kind of your role.
But you sparkle because you're clear, crystal and
fragile, like glass.
You might be cracked now, but it will not last.

RUNNING AWAY FROM ME

Sometimes when something bad has happened I retreat
into a past state; I repeat the past hate.
I've got no control, can't help it -
feels like I have no soul because this evil thing has
happened
and so I must deserve every second of this pain.
It's what causes me to act strange, act insane.
I needed to be told everything was gonna be okay,
it wasn't my fault, be nice to hear.
But people run from me, run in fear.
"You're fucked up, I don't want to know you,
I'd rather piss off than show you life can be worth living."
"I've got too much of my own stuff to sort, without giving
any attention to you.
But I'll update my facebook status and mention you."
Well done, point well made, doesn't change the fact that
I'm beginning to fade
and no one is here to come to my aid.
They've washed their hands because I've made
demands,
and the grains of sands in the timer are running out for
us.
I'll have to move on, in time, and start anew, something I
always have to do.
Just wish you could have seen past what I did or said,
because I was in pain, the mist was red, just like you
said.
'Til death do us part, so breaks my heart,
and things have been said, may as well be dead,
so I'm not gonna get out of bed.
I'll act just like a dead body, not moving because I've got
nobody.
Just put me to sleep, to sleep I wish to be,
because being awake, alone, is agony, unknown.

DON'T DESERVE ME AT MY BEST

If you can't ride the rollercoaster you won't be
getting the most out of me,
the best out of me, it's a test you see;
who's worth riding out the whole journey.
You think you're worthy? You gotta take the drops
and the shudders on the track,
you gotta think that there's no turning back.
I'm gonna make you feel dizzy and sick,
feel like you can't stick it.
I sometimes won't act myself and seem wicked and
wrong.
But that's just me; you have to be strong.
Before the deep low there's a magical show
that's amazing to be around.
You think you've found the best person ever,
amazing, smart, thoughtful and clever.
That's what you say about me.
Question is, will you stay with me when I fall?
Will you answer when I call?
I'm hard work, and that's understating,
someone you love or someone you will be hating.
But Marilyn Monroe was in the know when she
pointed out
you can't have the plus sides without the rough
rides.
You can't enjoy my good attributes and then ditch
me in disputes.
You don't deserve the coaster high if you're gonna
say goodbye when I drop to my knees.
I'm not just a showgirl, there to please;
I'm complex as you can get, probably more
complex than you've ever met.

I'm gonna make you laugh, and then I'll make you
cry,
you'll want to be my best friend and then you'll see
the torment,
you'll be so glad you met me then repent the day
you caught sight of me.
This is not doing right by me.
I'm a rollercoaster, highs and lows,
if you stick with me you'll know that it shows I'll get
back to top form right after the storm.
But you don't deserve to see me in all my glory,
if you close the book at the rough part of the story.
If you want the amazing high, you gotta take the
terrible low,
and if you deserve me, you gotta understand, you
gotta know.

ACCEPTANCE AND REMORSE

Okay, so the drone,
my double, my clone
speaks through me more than known before.
Thought meds could help it heal the sore,
but red the mist will make it raw.
Like a paper cut, must be nuts, when use these
knives as paper cuts.
The mist isn't red, it's black, once it's made known,
can't come back from fallen throne.
I regret what I say;
gonna do it anyway.
I say what I do in anger and hurt,
but the worst is said with passion, spitting through
love.
Just understand me and my ways.
The black mist hazes over me, the evil raises over
me.
I'm still here, but I've gone wrong,
my hand reaches out for another to grip and pull
me to shore.
Lifeboats? Out there, there's just one more.
Save me, I'll behave; don't put me in the grave,
six feet under, lightning and thunder,
will you forgive me, I wonder?
Here's my cry out, SOS, I confess now I need the
best.

ARE YOU GONNA STICK WITH ME?

You said you'd stick by me, forever, to the end;
only took a bend in the rule to have me looking like a
fool.
Things are destroyed; everyone is annoyed at me
because I lost my self,
 in grief and poor health.
I needed you to stick with me, but you're sick of me,
you've made a right prick of me and now the clock is
tock-tick for me.
Time's running out, I'm spinning out,
my hair is thinning now,
coming out in clumps when I'm tearing it,
and you're all sharing in swearing to tell me I've had my
last chance.
I tried to stay strong in my stance in this pathetic bicker;
but it's making me sicker.
Either you stand by me, or you go,
either give a hand to me or know,
you were never a true friend after all.
Bend, break, brittle, fall.
Are you with me or against me?
Are you my comrade or my foe? Do you really even
know?
I said what I said out of love, I'm not ashamed of it,
won't be blamed for it, so guess this is the end of the
game.
Such a fucking shame, thought ties were tough but they
turn out to be tame.
Very few are in my halls of fame of those that last,
very few, unlike you, will last.
Maybe you saved yourself and got out in time,
just before the shit hit the fan.
Or maybe, guys, you could have stuck with the plan.
You hit the road, did one, ran. You never will stick it,
never could or can.

CALL ME AN AMBULANCE

So today I'm on a low and it shows;
who knows if it stays or goes.
I'm as needy as you can get, yet as speedy to regret
my actions, and there is little or no satisfaction,
and definitely no distraction.
I've been wrong and maybe deserve some punishment,
but more importantly I need some nourishment.
I need to feed my breaking heart for it to restart
pumping.
My heart has stopped and my head is thumping
and so help jump start it for your part.
Some people are showing me support that I can't
ignore,
but I'm lacking the presence of those I adore.
This doesn't feel right, my chest is tight, can't breathe,
can't relieve my restricted airways,
can't spend my days like this.
Tell me what I need to do,
to help me pull through.
Put me on a drip,
so the goodness can slip into my veins
and ease my many pains.
The pain of loss, the pain of cost,
the frost bite that has bitten my toes,
can't keep my feet on the ground.
I'm deaf, I can't hear the sound of happy voices all
around.
I've got no doctor, got no nurse,
just getting worse and worse.
So where are you all?
I've had a fall.
Help me up, pick me up off the floor.
I can't do this, I can't take it anymore.

BURNING AT THE STAKE

Ok, so now I'm getting obsessed,
so I'll say it once more before I give it a rest.
You are burning me at the stake;
just because I didn't want to act fake.
I need you, need you guys,
I'm crying my eyes out here,
I'm sighing the lies away,
just forgive me, okay?
I'm not a bad girl,
sometime's I'm a whirlwind,
a force of great destruction,
crumble buildings in the eruption of my will.
I got hurt by someone, and it makes me ill.
Makes me take it out on everyone I love;
so please see above all this rubble.
I'm stuck within a bubble and
I'm in a lot of trouble and I'm completely on my one.
Help me pop it so I can be the me that's fun.
This is my last cry for help, my attention-seeking
plea.
Can't you see that ignoring me is destroying me?
What did I do? Stab you? Rape you? Hurt you?
All I did was show I won't desert you.
I said what I thought was best for you
and you've made into a test that's meant I've lost.
It will be at your own cost;
you won't ever find another friend like me.
A friend that has love to send like me.
Why are you turning away from me?
Why you burning me at the stake?
Just for one simple mistake of shouting at you.
I wasn't doubting you, I was trying to guide.
I've lost everything now, even my pride.

What I'm trying to say is I miss you,
so don't dismiss me.
Can't you reminisce on the good times we shared?
Can't you remember how you cared?
I've lost everything in losing you.
You probably think it's amusing too.
 I'm gonna sleep and hope this is over when I
wake.
 I'm gonna go to sleep now, burning at the stake.

POWER OF THREE

So the witch was burned at the stake,
but returned, the maker
put back the ashes to bake her form
and in it came the hell-blown storm.
By the power of replacing three
you will suffer for what you've done to me.
You watched the fire, then run from me;
you cast the stones whilst bearing sin
now the power comes from inside, within
to the night bird and his absurd bastard whore.
You wait and see what is in store;
you hurt me more than you can think of
now I'll bring you on the brink of the end.
Your days have been happy, happy to spend,
my money on you, happy to give my energy
to you, but there was no remedy for
the cruelty of nature, the trees and the wood
mirrored cruelty and smoke in glass.
You could never have understood
and it will come to pass
that your wretched ways
will be stretched in days
and you will have no release,
no solace or peace.
You hurt me more than those who drew out blood
you brought the fire, you gathered the wood
the coal, brought a torch
to watch me scorch,
but I resurrect and can correct
your punishment is direct.
By the power of the Moon and Sun;
so the magic becomes so done
The power of three, power of three.
He loses her, she loses him, they both lost me.

HAPPY BIRTHDAY DAD

Grey hairs appear in my hair;
genetically, phonetically I am his heir.
He is Mr Toad, poop-pooping down the road,
can shift into sensible mode when he has his wig
and cloak,
can all stigma revoke when you see he is a man of
high class,
but when put to the task, a man of the people.
Helped so many,
would give his last pound and his last penny,
man so kind, but man of such mind nothing he can't
teach me,
nowhere he can't reach me, to pick me up. Here
comes my father,
the one I'd rather be with, my true idol,
and like his own, he is a lone ranger,
feels stranger to himself, and doubts his power and
wealth.
But I'm proud of you, my dad, though I know I make
you sad.
You want the best for me and trust me the rest of
me
will keep going, because knowing I am your blood
keeps me fighting.
Wrongs I'll keep righting because I am the blood
line,
so there's my sign that justice prevails, because of
all the tales
of his mastery, his history and I am proud to be
raised.
My father is praised by me,
I want you to see that, father, I love you with all my
heart,

you are the best part of me.
You are my family.
I'll do my best, dad,
I'll fight, I'll save, I'll always be brave,
I'll try to do right.
I'll even put on the wig and gown and stand in court,
because I'm your daughter
and I'm so glad to be.
I might be mad, you see, but so are you.
Are we mad really? We are two.
I'll grit my teeth and pace towards the face of the ugly, be it good or bad.
You're the man with no name, but you're my dad.
I'll wear the poncho proud, and I'll shout out loud
He's David Leathley, barrister at law; he is my maker, my muse and more.
I'm such a mystic river that sometimes I don't deliver.
I don't seem to be glad to be his gene.
But I guess it's how I've ever survived all I've seen.
Might be an irritation to you, but I'm the creation of you.
This is a 44 Magnum pointed at you punk!
And this poem MIGHT be junk,
but make my day?
Just have a happy birthday.

BATTLING THE BEAST

Okay, I have some more to say,
a bitter lesson to learn, about myself and my health, and what to say
and how to respect earn in every single way.
I still have this beast inside of me over which I feel I have no control,
takes my body,

steals my tongue and leaves me behind.
I have good attributes; I'm kind and you may have
known me in many ways,
a worthless bitch or a girl to praise,
or just heard how I spent my days.
When the beast takes control, it's a force above me
that hurts the most the ones who love me.
If someone is hurting the ones I love, beast has no
pause,
bares its claws and ignores all warning to run to
attack.
I will, without warning, stab you in the back.
I am a beast that has a pack, and my pack I love
dearly, but it's not clear to me,
why I disappear and make them fear.
This beast inside of me is because of those who've
bruised, used, lied to me.
Guess it's my subconscious guiding me, but
sending people away
and ending up in this lost place.
It's the burden, the beast I have to face.
I'll love you like a deer just born to the earth,
defend you like walls and with all my worth,
until all my talking can see your weakened legs
walking.
I gallop in a herd, and then the release of a word
has them powering away from me,
I drive them not to stay with me.
Then it leaves me like this.
I'm not to be trusted, my armour has rusted
and all I wanted was to keep you close.
Keep my little birds in my nest, not this test of who will
stick.
I've got love in here, but the wounds are thick.
I'll have to start again, just as I did then,

find a V-shaped flight in the sky to see if I can with
join with them and fly.
It breaks my heart every time
and I whip myself in remorse for letting life run its
course
because that's what it's gotta be?
I'm finding out my destiny; who will rest with me.
It's just a test, building your own nest.
When the beast is dead, then will I be reborn?
 Or will I be nothing, broken and torn.
God help me, give me a sign?
Is it just nature or is it your design
That I'm not learning this lesson? Do I not have you're
blessing?
I can be a beast, but also your friend,
just don't know where it starts and where it ends.
Now once again I have to defend,
speak now, for I am weak now, if you have hope to
lend?

THE RIPPLE EFFECT

The ripples that run on and on,
and then you are gone.
When pebble in water drops and scatters thoughts
and gets on top
The water, so settled, the reflection of a
resurrection,
the pool that is cool to bathe and calm,
will save you from harm from the fire.
Walk on water, give into your desire.
But alter the surface of liquid glass,
bully, abuse, harass creates the ripple effect
and makes life incorrect.
Don't create an explosion; it causes corrosion in my
little pond.
It causes me to break, hate and beyond.
Causes me to take, berate, and I am a fond to
many
until the ripple sends me to the any land
where the demand is to self destruct;
Pollute the water and corrupt.
The ripple effect can connect me to bad forces and
divorce me from all my friends.
The ripple effect can be brief or never end.
Never ending means you're sending me to the sea,
where I am pushed down river and cease to be.
If you've got a net in my water, baiting me, you may
as well be creating the end.
My waves will rock your boat, so take note and
defend yourself by not trying to drown me.
I need good people around me
For I am stagnant, so much pollution, and there is
no solution in antagonizing me.
It is agonizing, you see.

The ripple effect is stronger than you think, pushes people to the brink,
through drink, drugs, gets them involved with thugs and then you sink.
The change in tide can even lead to death and suicide.
So please, keep me healthy, for you know that I am ill.
 Please, I implore thee, don't ignore me, and keep my waters still.

HEAL ME, I'M POSSESSED

Heal me, heal me
you can't keep stealing me.
I don't belong to you anymore, I don't belong, that I'm
sure.
I want to follow the path of the right,
I want to write now of how this thing takes hold of me,
messes with the mould of me.
I have to be bold or give in to my grief.
I have to stop giving into the thief.
Regret, remorse, I keep getting on course and then the
force
of evil, and hate, and anger, and the monster, my taker.
People think I am a faker,
but this is still my burden to bear,
my chains that I wear
my damnation. I am damned.
my soul in remand,
what's next? What's planned?
What do I need to learn or lose
to prove to you that I have good to use?
I can channel energy, and it can be blinding with its
power
can last seconds, minutes, hours.
I can help you, redeem you, give you the best
or I can destroy, and give you the test.
And nobody should have to deal with me.
The regret is very real and see
I pray to be forgiven,
I pray them not to be driven away,
I'll pray to the higher, every day.
Heal me, heal me,
don't reveal yourself, possessor.
I am the regretting, damned confessor.

MIKA

Thespian friend of mine, your drama defined, every
little word or wit is comedian and every bit a
shooting star, you are routing far into the sky,
there's been no casualty in your reality, oh wait,
weren't you one of the extras?
In your trade you are so dexterous. Your sing-song
voice gives me to the choice to smile and compile
each note to my devotion to you. When you sing
you bring eyes to wide, you've got so much talent
and love inside. Never shows rage, unless it's
required of the stage. You wrap your arm around
me and the charm confounds me that you are
always so understanding, even when faced with a
case so demanding such as mine. You make me
think everything will be fine, you're the Pink Floyd
(even if this makes others annoyed) you're the Brad
Pitt, the Johnny Depp; you make me feel less inept.
You are my friend and I hope you're kept. One day,
you will be a King Lear, appearing in Shakespeare;
be Dick van Dyke if you like. If you want to view
paradise... like Gene Wilder sang, you've always
been part of my gang. I believe you could do Doctor
Who; it's the role made for you, because you're a
time traveller, because you've remained in my life
for years. Laughed, listened, wiped my tears and I'll
forever be your fan. Because you are my film star,
and you can.

THE LYNCH MOB

Here comes the lynch mob to get me. So come with
your torches;
you won't upset me. It tortures me with regret that
it's come to this
and I'll hear your fires burning, crackling hiss.
All I'll do is miss the good times before you
committed such crimes against me.
Maybe I deserve it, maybe I'm perverted,
but I thought you were worth it, once upon a time,
 you gave me your love once and I gave you mine.
The mob is coming, I'm not running,
there's nothing to run from, not when you come
from where I've been
and what I've seen.
I regret my weakness but I'm trying to clean up my
act,
be a good person, and that's a fact.
I've said sorry, time and time again.
It won't ever be enough, I accept,
it's torture enough just to reflect.
I'm driven away by myself not you,
I'm driven to other places and ventures new.
Put on your hoods, you haven't quite understood
me,
get the coal, matches, wood and come see me
burn like the wicker man,
I'm slicker than that. I don't wanna bicker like that.
I want to be strong and I am, so come for me, if you
can,
come, try, carry me away with the pack.
I regret what I said and it's compassion you lack.
He who is without sin cast the first stone;
I have developed, risen, grown.

Hands reach at me to grab at me, have a stab at me.

I'll be strong and won't do the wrong thing and react,

you haven't got me, I haven't cracked.

ANGEL FISH

I'm starting fresh again, and I'm a different wave
in this sea of murky water and revenge, regret and
fear
I no longer want to save anyone not worth saving
and I'll start behaving because the water's running
clear.
Like the flow of the pump in my fish aquarium that I
like to sit and look at,
the water's being filtered and if you took energy
from me, or simply shook the tank,
I forgive you and I know now it's you I gotta thank.
You're teaching me lessons that my soul is learning
and I'm earning my place in the world, or in the
next.
Things are gonna drag you under that you can't
really expect.
But I'm gonna rise above it, above sea level,
won't be dishevelled and won't let the abuse make
me more confused.
I'm gonna be the Angelfish and I'm gonna stop
being used.
People see into my reef and coral, lack the morals,
then I have a thief in my bank account, my body,
my time,
you start making me acidic because of the tank
amounts of lime.
The waters are dangerous and I'm a direct victim of
the ripple effect
and you can't swim with me.
The school of little fishes leave nasty little wishes
and swim together away
and back to their bitter pool.
 If you didn't stay with me

and had harsh words to say to me
 then you are the fool.
Because the sands of time are settling at the
bottom of the sea,
and I am a good person, and it was you clouding it
for me!
Nobody deserves to be stung by my sting, and it's
not something I am proud of,
but I don't need you crowding my lake of tranquil
submersion.
This is the conversion of me. No more negativity.
Just gonna leave it be.
I'm going to breathe underwater and just be born a
daughter new.
 I'm done with your fishing nets, I don't need you.

FORGIVE/ FORGET – THE WHITE BIND

Forgive, forget,
let's heal and set a new vibration humming through
the plane,
this sensation is coming through the pain.
No more. No more. Let's restore the damaged
crops,
let's wipe the wooden floors with many mops,
let's rise above and be on top. Let's get soppy
when we think that life is really worth living
and sincerely send these positive spirits giving,
good thoughts, good vibes,
describes how things will pick up.
I will lick up the salt I poured on you.
I'll get some tippex, erase, undo.
And yes, this will be ignored by those I've wounded
and hissed at,
people I was twisted and pissed at,
but now I send you good wishes,
We got a lot of dishes to do,
I'll wash, and I'll dry,
I'm not gonna cry, I'll just wish you well.
I'll undo the spell, cast a new one where a white
bind wraps around you and is kind
and gets you through.
The white bind is binding me too.
 Forgive, forget, we will see joy soon, just not yet.

KODAC MOMENT SHIT

I'm trying to be someone better than I am, can roll
back the film on the camera and can take other
pictures of other Kodac moment shit. There are
other scriptures to read and more targets to hit.
There's more times to laugh and more of the wit
and the just giggling at someone's face and I'm
wriggling through to that place, picking up the ace
in ring of fire and worse having the last king and
then you can disregard everything 'cause you
KNOW you'll be sick, face up to it, lost the race up
to it, so down the drink quick. Quicksand can't stop
the summer coming, even if it lasts just a few days,
nothing can stop the haze of smoking in a room,
and nothing really ever means doom. You can have
a destiny, but just test to see if you can change it
first. There will be other snapshots of smiles on
your Facebook page. Facebook has a timeline, so I
guess it, too, will age. You are always gonna think
the worst but there's always a Kodac moment in the
pipe line, so just look through the lens and capture
the sign.

THING IS, I LOVE YOU

Things are a little fuzzy when I think, 'Does he think of me at all?', especially when he's seen the brink of my disaster. You just roll your eyes at my demise, tell me to put a plaster on it and get over it. You see me fall over, and soon it's all over and you have not got the patience to put up with it. Our conversation is awkward and I am clumsy, chat shit, so thick with the sensation of it. I remember the time and I wonder if you think of it at any point, I am joined to you at the hip even though you look at the lips you once kissed and are clearly dismissing me. You are ashamed of this and you're usually pissed at me. I give you a headache with all the mistakes I make and to be honest you've been less give and more take more often. So why is it that I soften when I see you? There is something that pulls me in and I'm so curious, you usually end up snapping at me, furious. There really is no point for me trying to play it cool, thing is I love you, so I act twice the fool. My palms are sweaty, waiting for you to come get me, I'm gonna stammer and try make some small talk, but I reckon you'll always walk away from me. Anything I thought you felt is a trip, not real, an illusion, so I should get over this delusion to avoid more confusion. But thing is, I adore you completely and you ignoring defeats me. But there's still something there. I know that some small spark in your heart cares. Thing is, I love you, are you aware?

LITTLE BIRDS AND THEIR WORDS

Little birds and their little words mean nothing, they can't peck open your heart for a start, but they are still a part of nature and what is both loving and cruel. My words have created a pool of blood that is red, bright red, not what you said... never blue and repentance has been felt where it's due for what I said to you. Little birds flapping, dancing in the trees, slapping anger out of me and romancing my fire, so there is no more desire to lash out. I've had a crash, and hit the wall, I've been falling and now I've landed back at the home tree. Little birds are seeing sense you see. I hope you can feel past tense, and pity. I was once a little bird in the city and there were many flapping around me, my wings have been taken and therefore ground me, so confound what little birds of stupidity sang at you that day, they are paying for it. The words are ringing in their ears, and this little bird has cried many tears for saying it. Little birds can peck out your eyes, so you don't see what you should, but little birds can't alter your heart and never could.

LIFE IN SUSPENSION – WRITER'S BLOCK

I've got a bit of writer's block, must have been the knock, the shock to the system, means I can't impart any wisdom. I'm feeling more than a bit isolated out of the situation I created and now I've got to stop and rewind. There's something I have to find. I have learnt already that I can't act on impulse, I have to stop the convulse of emotions surging through me because there's a purging quality to the urging fit which means now I'm solitary with the aftermath of it. I'm wrapping a scarf around my head, wearing sunglasses so my eyes are not read, in hiding. I'm to each law abiding, not breaking free with the mania glee, but in a complete state of self-reflection. Suppose I have to be, seeing as I've lost my connections. But now I'm wondering if I'm missing some direction, something that's gonna show me the way. I'm gonna miss it if I'm in hiding all day. Or maybe I just need to carry on turning the key and lock myself in. But I'm yearning to see if there's a knock that I'll win and stay standing when it hits me. I'm trying on new faces to see which one fits me. Right now the one I wear is one of peace and calm. I'm pinning down the rage and harm. Thing is, I just want to be able to write, but it's a bit difficult when there's nothing in sight but the clock, ticking the moments I'm not seeing away, I've got writers block from being away. You can't just look inward; you've got to look outward too. It is only ever exciting when it includes you too. Can't think... guess I'll just wait 'til the others are inviting. I'm all out of ink, can't do any writing.

DEAD FLOWERS

What do you do with dead flowers? They had so
many powers, so many hours ago. They bloomed
once in your gloom, but petals and scent are dry
and gone, cry over colours that once shone, like
dying lovers who embrace no longer meant it, pull
the covers tight around you, pretend you dreamt it,
the flowers again surround you and extend, the
beds of flowers are on the mend, lay on the bed
which does not shed lies, be born again, and arise,
the ground is fertile and vast, rays of light exist, not
overcast with mist like today. Don't dwell over dead
flowers and keep doubt at bay. Cut off their heads,
and walk away. Others will grow, soon you will
know, and gardens of greatness will never go.

EMPATHY

There's people who will, without a doubt,
know what you're about,
there's people who will not question you;
maybe have a suggestion or two, but will listen,
and accept you.
These people are special, they detect you, and
come forward to empathise;
won't laugh, mock or criticise.
There's always some out there. Some who, without
conditions, will care.
Calling without commissions, they're aware -
maybe because they once had the same cross to
bear,
maybe they're just amazing,
and now, of course my eyes are glazing, glistening
with the thought of those who have understood me,
they've been the best they could be.
I can't thank you enough,
I've banked a good moment in time,
been bankrupt
in this world so corrupt.
But I think I'll be fine...
Thanks to you, for understanding,
in this world so demanding.
You lent a hand and pulled me up to stand.

SPECK

I am a speck within a crowd,
whispering out loud, moving too quick for the eye to see,
passing me by so utterly,
without noticing, without a clue,
that here I am, watching you.
Moving, moving, unmoving I am.
I remain black pearl in tightly shut clam.
At the bottom of the ocean, a million miles away
and I've been here the whole time,
 not knowing what to say.
Different world, different words, reality absurd.
Reality is mad at me, and I am sad to be stuck between paths
in a unsympathetic tearful aftermath.
I've felt the hand of God and I am fearful of his wrath,
but creatures in between, with features of the hated
remain unseen,
and morbidly fated.
Spinning on its axis, like London lit up with many taxis,
I've trying to hitch a lift, but I've lost power, lost the gift,
Lost the hours, speeding life, speeding fast,
and here I am, still stuck to the past.
Look again, train in a tunnel and everything goes black.
It's me, right here, wanting you back.
Corner of your eye, blink, you've missed it, shrink,
shrinking I've fixed it,
couldn't use tape to tie you to me, saying goodbye goes
through me
shudder, shiver down the spine,
it's just me, wishing you were mine.
Look between journeys, look closer, I'm right here
waiting in smoke for you to appear.

SOFTLY SPOKEN

Jumping back, in fright, I suddenly catch sight of
the meaning of this,
eyes bright, but softly spoken, soft are the lips
and in the way of the sun, eclipsed is my mind,
and breaking, unmaking is the bind, the devotion,
as all we were, everything, a notion.

MOLEY THE PROCLAIMED

Life's all about those little moments when you are
reminded there is someone kind of heart
who's always been close yet far apart.
A true friend, little messages that mend and he's
always had the time to send.
Proclaiming true heart and a thousand miles, for a
start you've surfed through my drama
with shield and armour saying, 'Harm her and I'll rip
your nose off' (but I laugh 'cause he shows off).
Wears his heart in your face because normally has
clothes off, but his worth is as clear as his nipple
ring.
So hope good surf is what life brings ya.
Chase some bulls, fights some bears,
someone here cares about you, and will do,
always.
The days we used to have, and I'm proud of the
ones you're having now,
here's my friend,
cracking me up again, backing me up again
somehow.

I CAN'T SEE THE STARS

Clouds divide me from my pride, as I see no stars;
now stormy night
and the tide bellows broken glass, lost sight of the
task
and it makes you ask,
'Why are we?'
'We are because we are,' and so then wait for night
that's starry.
So if you've travelled far, or you've yet to see a star
there's a door to go through, one to find -
you've only to open it to leave this behind.
Set off in hope, in blindness grope along the walls
until the handle does appear
Don't stall, or be stranded, just because tonight's
sky is not clear.

BECOME THE EARTH

Chase up the mountain, meet the sun in the sky, on
top of the earth
no longer shy, give birth to the strength within
feel your own soft skin
turn into textured bark
your hands clutch rays
away from the dark
remember the days of play when you were a child
become a force among the wild
your feet dig routes sinking deep to the ground
twisting as you are existing in nature found
wait for it, wait for the light
be comforted, the future's bright.

LIVE

Watch the colours morph, transcend before your
eyes,
shut lightly, mend, expect not surprise
delicate, soothing, blissful, calm
removing, wishful, and with peace, embalm.
This time, the moment that you notice you are truly
alive
is the moment you notice you might actually
survive.

SPITEFUL TOXIN

Oh spiteful toxin, from thee I divorce,
I shall no longer give shoulder, protect or endorse,
and I feel no pain in parting,
nor shame or remorse,
now I truly see thee,
most corrupting the force.

SOLDIER ANTS

Little soldier ants, working, lifting leaves together
marching through raindrop crystals, endeavour
to keep marching, strong as the ground,
speedy, resources in built to nature, not found.
I'll try to join you
and I'll try conjoin to
this world to cherish but labour in, we're bound.

DAWN'S HEALING LIGHT

The warmth and sensation vibrating in creation of
the source of healing and light,
breathe through the feeling and force, hold tight,
just like portrait hangs on wall slanted,
you are being realigned and granted permission to
let yourself out remission.
Just for today, say:
don't worry and let go,
rise not to rage and compassion show.
Turn the page, get well,
meditate and grow...

THEY

They are always with you
when days are bleak, keeping you strong,
walking with you on journeys long.
They will seek to lift you up when you are drifting
embrace the energy within you shifting as
Angel comes with power to guide you through
such weary hour.
Harmony found, no longer bound
you can take flight!
...and with new found might
you can borrow some wings...
Now see what today brings :)

LOOK UP

So you've fallen over, hit the ground,
worry not as you have found
the way back, it's simply above
look up, you are sent love.

THE CHANNEL

I had a glimpse of my own ending
but the channel of energy bending
you are the path to your own mending
with angel love, light they're sending.

BECAUSE WHEN I CRY

Because when I cry it erupts emotions deep
and, like awakening from sleep,
I can see the breaking morning new
I remember life is beautiful too

MY FRIEND

If they're your friends, they'll come back.
Perhaps perspective is what I've lacked
and sure enough, now time is due
I see my friend; my friend is you.

INDIGO HEART

Indigo heart, one that is pure and virgin again
feel your power surging and then
release all the old flames that melted thy
candle of the past, ask yourself why
they didn't last
become woman strong, but woman ready and open
to
all the possibilities of love before you...

THE PLACE

Walk toward the place, your feet tripping over you
with every break
of gripping excitement to be one with the force,
hands shake,
no indictment or remorse, for the life that you've
been leading,
only humility and with your whole self pleading
to be at one with this cosmic climactic vibration
of nature, not just intact with the nation
but you send hope to those that you've mixed with,
hope that their own problems can be fixed, and give
your energy back to the Earth, and for those who
walk it
I'm speaking of my rebirth, and I'm gonna talk a bit
of ecstasy, but not the chemical kind,
the belonging, the commemorative bind
to everything, and yourself you will find
something, look ahead not behind

THE DESIGN

Can't tolerate it, I've been trying to consolidate it,
there's been too much of a wait for the strength to
contemplate or the wondering and then nature is
thundering with all its voice, and you're clearly
showing me the choice that you're not that way
inclined so even if we are designed to celebrate I
will compensate that you don't deserve me, and I
deserve someone worthy, and like vitamins and
scurvy, I am nourishment and serve thee but you
back away, ashamed of what you feel, and it's not
worth exploring what you yield to because your own
doubt deserts me and I will back out before you
hurt me, you had the choice, you knew what it's
worth, but nothing brought you back down to earth,
and your always looking for something better than
what you've found, so go for it, but I'm more
profound.

I can't actually take it, the ways you can fake it and
enjoy pretending to and I'm amending you to be the
man you want to be for the girls that you want so
happily, you want to be this man above standard,
and nothing you planned would go exactly like you
thought it out, and you're hoping that someone
would just kinda 'sort you out', put you in touch with
the ending, wouldn't be much point, in defending
your actions, but it would mean your own
satisfactions and so if not mine, it's clear my
design, try to make you happy and make everything
fine, but I hope you know that you're a bit
shortsighted, suppose to do the right thing, you'd

have to be knighted but you didn't see it so who cares, can't be caught unawares, I thought you were dreams but you're really nightmares.

Show me the release, before you send me police, you thought that I'd probably give up and cease to be the girl that you want, I am part of a world that you aren't and now I'm a person at peace so move on and don't hurt, for the growth and the spurt you can trouble divert till the day it reverts to you back to your mission, you need to tackle suspicion 'til you can see premonitions and be on top of position so get stronger, last longer, just sing your own song. You didn't want me, but sometimes we are wrong.

UNDERSTANDING

Open up your mind to new possibilities
find that responsibilities are present but not
demanding
come to new and wise understanding
you are able to do what you always planned to
if you can't understand this, just understand you.

THRIVE

If you think you're dead inside, you are only
sleeping,
so don't spend hours weeping over a grave that's
not filled
don't spend your time mourning a death that didn't
happen, build
an idea, see the dawning sun and let it wake you
up
don't let the warnings stun you so you're not taking
life up
on its offer, its gift, its opportunities
find some unity with the world that you are ALIVE in
and it will start being a world you will thrive in.

FIX UP

If the world hasn't loved you, don't let it make you
bitter
if you've run away from things, don't feel like a
quitter
Don't know people will hurt you, it's not a complete
fact
the problem isn't you, but it might be how you act.

TO YOU A SURVIVOR

Don't think for a second that this is your reckoning,
it's just a moment with all time beckoning,
you've stood so tall, been an inspiration to all
so don't think that having a fall means that this is it,
just means that it's life, and you're living it.
Just think about all the giving you gave, all the lives
that you saved
before you thought of your own, more than anything
you've shown
that you're the survivor, the thriver that has put life
back in the lost,
with no account for yourself, and thoughtless of the
cost
it has to your health, being a public figure
all your bravery, honesty and vigour,
the way you fight oppression, prejudice and stigma
whilst maintaining such curiosity, you beautiful
enigma,
you will rise again as sure as tomorrow will
today I am strong, for you it's to borrow 'til
you're keeping me strong like you always have done,
the right that has wrongs written off and undone,
you will rise again, as sure as the sun rises,
but that's not your mystery, carries no surprises.
Because you survive, it is your position,
this is just your waiting, your bit in remission
until you eclipse, take over the night,
just remember it's coming, soon... hold tight.

POSITION IN AMBITIONS

your position in ambitions is just your situation
it is not your final word, end or creation,
and even if you've taken some recreation,
on the path to getting a standing ovation
don't regret or fear the invitation,
or regret the drop, the effect of temptation
just see it as a pretty good combination,
hindsight and experience, stands apart from a
nation
creates such reflective contemplation
you can identify and detect your damnation
to prevent and deflect act imitation
to begin and reflect moral invention,
to relieve anxiety, worries and tension,
that you can prohibit, fight with prevention,
a life that continues, without a redemption
you can give yourself time, grant an extension,
'til you take control of your acts and intentions.

TO A SOLDIER'S FAMILY

Having the strength and belief to carry on just living
when soldiers march into but not out of war,
but just existing through the pain is giving
so much greater, bigger, more.
Just be strong, stay strong for each other
families are tied with chords and they have not
undone your brother, your son.
He is still wrapped around you, holding you all
together,
he'll still be a soldier, with hand upon your shoulder,
now into forever
as your hero, your guide,
He still is with you, our nation's pride.
Some of us have so small a time upon this plane,
suffer short the pain of this, and it's insane to
analyze why this happened to you, why it could
happen, why it did to yours.
Just know that your family adores each member,
and know he is not only just to remember, but he'll
be walking with you and guiding you now, please
find this on your path to deciding on how you are
strong. Love is eternal, and never wrong.
You will get through this. You will get through this.
Nothing anyone wouldn't give just to undo this;
but remember the chord that binds you close with
love means he's now your mentor, from above.
Call on him to give you strength when you are weak
in the eye of the storm. Your soldier that once so
bravely performed for our country, with altruistic
flare, will be with you always, everywhere.

A champion, a lord, a saviour, a knight,
is arm in arm with the angels tonight,
and his example takes breath away, his memory an
inspiration
has today become the creation of respect
as we all salute him and expect
his award for his service to his ancestors, his nation,
his loved ones, to you.
he'll be rewarded with angels, and will be the light
shining through.

HALL OF CHAMPIONS

I'm burning a candle, praying for you,
hoping that I can repay something to you.
I'm holding you tight in my thoughts and lifting you
from this,
and I wish that you could see the promise that is
there for you.
It's bound in love and everyone's prayer for you.
A light appears over your household.
A dent in the sky of a million-year-old strength
illuminating from the length of might
that is keeping you together tonight.
An angel, one from the right-hand seat of the Lord,
raises his sword in honour so high,
and it has left a blue tattoo in the sky.
Let every tear that you cry empower you greatly,
so that you can later see how you are the bloodline
of something deeper and more profound
than the rest of us poor people who still put foot to
ground.
In the hall of champions he is seated
like old friends reunited, greeted,
and they celebrate his achievement,
but honour the bereavement.
They tell him that all that he has done will be given
reward,
and just at that moment the angel hands him his
sword
and says, "Fear not, my brother.
You are set apart from the others.
You went out protecting
so this we're directing to those you left behind."
The angels of service have set out to find you.

They cannot rewind and undo it,
but they will push you forward, and get you through
it.
A great feast in the heavens sings out in tribute,
but among the celebration, a soldier in suit,
looks down upon the sky and raises high his bright
sword
of mighty brilliance and blue,
it reaches out and joins the light below,
connected to you.

RISE OF THE PHOENIX

And so, I broke free from the ashes and the demons
that held
like magnetic force, I broke free and repelled
and to rise again, from the abyss of black
felt like coming home, like coming back,
but I was different, better, something had changed in
me,
and I saw all the spectrum of possibility ranged in me
the ability I had to be strong, be stronger than I had
been,
and it was like a stranger looking on what's been done
and seen,
it appeared that change was clear in my resurrection
powers had stepped in, of right and correction,
and this was unlike all the other times I've flown.
I had been in chrysalis, developed and grown,
and it was like awakening from sleep for the first time in
years
something had soothed, me settled my fears.
I was strong, I am strong, I've been strong
and everything I'd done, even what was wrong
has all been a test, to see if I deserved the insight,
and spreading my hopes and wings, took flight.
Life could bring anything and I'd be ready for it,
I could be a survivor, instead of
a victim, I can handle the world that we live in
and I was no longer recoiled in reliving
the paths that I has walked, and this delivering
a new bit of sight that appeared on my crown
I would look to the sky and never back down
I was a piece of the earth, nature's child
no longer felt outcast, creature of the wild
I'd been living in regret, and riddled with my past
I knew to embrace the future, it's happening fast.

THE GOLDEN AGE

This year is going to be the best year ever,
the unthinkable is happening, the forgotten, the never,
people predicted it ending, looking at the blank page,
in fact it's the changing, the coming golden age,
You have to be optimistic, forget realistic,
it's going to be incredible, forget cataclysmic
and you don't have to pay attention to religion or science
the point is for freedom, not global compliance,
this year brings beauty for many to see,
to break free from the barriers your mind must be free.

THE RIPPLE EFFECT

If something happens to you at any point in your life that is damaging, you can observe the consequent effect on your behaviour, mental health and personality. People become negative people because they are labelled, hurt, abused, or have suffered life events that change their perception of themselves and the world. This can be any sort of stressor, such as verbal, physical or sexual abuse, bereavement, a knock-back in work, or the end of a relationship. It is so easy to take on board the negativity of the external world and internalise it in yourself. It is, of course, a natural thing to accept and go through the process of what and why this has happened, especially with bereavement; you cannot shrug everything off, but it is important not to internalise it.

We all must protect ourselves against the feeling that it is our fault, or because of us that these things happen. Imagine a pool of tranquillity in a beautiful setting. Visualise it in your mind... perhaps the birds are singing, perhaps a weeping willow lets its leaves hang lethargically over it, perhaps the sky is blue and clear. This pool is calm and purifying. If someone drops a stone into the pool, it disturbs the setting and everything that the pool embodies. The water, the fish, the plants within are disturbed and the ripples set loose from the disruption have an effect on everything. We are all one of these pools - the ripple effect can happen to all of us.

The stone dropping into the pool is a fact of life and we cannot always stop it; it's how we control the ripples that matters. It is important not to let the disturbance continue for your whole life. Accept the disturbance in your tranquillity, but let the water of calm reform and become serene again. It is up to us to let this process happen. We must stay strong and know we are forces of good. Otherwise, it's as though the stone bounces off the water and repeatedly creates more ripples. Let the stone go into the pond so it is accepted and settles; let the event or stressor be accepted and taken as it is.

One of the most important things is to understand the disturbance in others, to understand there are reasons behind the ripples; there are reasons behind the behaviour. Otherwise it is just as if you are dropping more and more stones into the pond. We must show consideration to other people and their behaviour - there are always reasons behind it. In the reflection of my own pool, the bullying, rejection and betrayals of others led me down the path of becoming bitter and hating the world. The reaction of other people, calling me bitter and hateful, only created more ripples. I'm not going to say that I didn't make choices that made it worse, but sometimes we are misguided, and if something happens to us, then we cannot really be expected not to. The only way to change this is to change ourselves, and not become passive products of other people. We must believe in our own ability to handle the situations, to not become passive products of them.

THE PERILS OF MEPHEDRONE

I want to speak from experience here, and send out a warning - though it is up to others if they take it on board. Mephedrone (cat, Mkat, Meow, Drone, Meph, Magic) is one of the newest and probably the most popular drugs on the scene at the moment. It is sweeping the world. If you have not heard of it, it began life as a legal high that was available on the internet. It is crystals that can be crushed into powder, has a very distinct smell, and is usually snorted through the nose. Mephedrone appears to be the best drug most people have ever had. It is between the experience of cocaine and ecstasy, with more euphoria than cocaine and more control than ecstasy. It truly puts you on a level of understanding and closeness with people, and you form friendships on an intimate level. For me, it was my social crutch, the blanket masking my insecurities about who I was, and the booster for my mania, meaning the attractive and socially powerful person I was came out.

The frightening thing about mephedrone is that you stay up for much longer than you ever have before on a drug binge, with my early sessions lasting about three days, but later sessions in the midst of all my mental health problems, insomnia and dreary surroundings being eight days long. I literally watched all my friends have complete breakdowns because of it, with the sleep and food withdrawal making everything stranger and stranger. It begins with the overall feeling of peace and love towards others, but it is an illusion, quickly turning to aggression and sadness.

Mephedrone is horrendously more-ish and the 'sessions' you begin you never want to end, because reality is such a terrifying and daunting thing to someone dependent on mephedrone. Mephedrone is an injection of life, love and spirit into your life, and reality is too much to take after taking it. It always begins as a few lines at a party, but eventually leads to you buying it to just keep going, to have the energy to do anything. It was particularly dangerous for me because I would seek it out when I was manic, so it prolonged the periods of insanity. I mentioned earlier that I started drug dealing again after I first got into mephedrone. Well, you would be surprised by the amount of people who do deal it now, and how young they can be. It starts off with a couple of grams, but your tolerance to it increases and, for me in particular and a lot of other people I know, you end up doing ounces of it every week. A gram of mephedrone is £15 and an ounce is about £200, so you can imagine what an expensive habit it becomes. You have to start dealing to maintain the amount of mephedrone that you are snorting, but this takes you into an even more frightening world.

You start off at the bottom of the chain, sorting mates out here and there and never really dealing with any nasty people. The more mephedrone you buy, the more it puts you in contact with heavier and more dangerous people. The 'big' men up the top of the chain are truly terrifying, evil people, whose lack of morals and lust for money and mephedrone makes them the most ruthless of all. Their mephedrone dependencies have rotted their brains completely, making them even more psychotic than their normal predispositions. If you are anywhere near this circle of darkness now, you must realize and get yourself out before you get involved with psychopaths or become one yourself. It is truly the most possessing and terrifying drug I've ever come across and it is astounding how many young people are involved in it. I believe more people who have been through the cycle of being enamoured with it, but have reached rock bottom and new lows should speak up, and let people know from the real perspective. Now, I'm no Christian, but the concept of the antichrist inspired me to write the poem 'The Drone', and it even says in the book of revelations 'the beast' is a cat. Mephedrone is the antichrist - will you be seduced by it?

THE WATER BEARERS

I'm taking things from a different perspective. A completely new vision, because that is what my life is guided by now: visions. I have always written poetry, and enjoyed writing in general, and always had a spiritual side, but never to this extent.

It is now that I believe that my poetry, both past and present, comes from the other side, is messages. I always tried to instil a moral in my poetry, and I'm not saying that a lot of it is not just my own creative streak. But I have experienced something in my recovery - well, why I DID recover. I can only tell you, but you will have to choose to believe. I realized that I am, have been all my life, an intensely spiritual person, with powers of divination and clairvoyance. I have been experiencing the realization of my own capability, of the worlds, of everybody, and now I choose to write about this, because simply, it is my life now.

Before I go on to explain myself a little further, I want to share my belief with you. This is through my own visions, premonitions, research and faith. The world is changing; we are entering a new realm.

"When the Moon is in the Seventh House, and Jupiter aligns with Mars, then Peace will rule the Planets, and Love will steer the Stars."

A lot of you will recognize that from the 1969 5th Dimension song 'Aquarius/ Let the sun shine in'. A lot of the younger generation will remember that from the film "The 40 Year Old Virgin". But jokes aside, it is happening. In 2012, we are experiencing a pole change. This is a scientific fact, but it is going be something much greater than that. The world will enter a new age and it means enlightenment for a lot of people, spiritual awareness and ability. It is age of happiness, peace, light and more importantly love. We must be ready for the change to accept it, to survive it, and I do believe that there will be a lot of loss, and disasters along the way. But I think, when the time comes, those of us who have love in our hearts can survive it and can go forth into the new age.

The astrology sign 'Aquarius' means 'The Water Bearer'. To me, the obvious symbol springs to mind: The Dolphin. The Dolphin, a mammal that lives under water, is a symbol of great peace, love and tranquillity worldwide. But what is the dolphin? He is the representation of water without being a fish, he is a part of the ocean and, more notably, the Dolphin has a very large brain and the ability to utilize all of it, setting it apart from us humans. This suggests that Dolphins may have abilities and powers that we, who only use less than a third of our brain, can only imagine. My belief is the Age of Aquarius will enlighten a lot of us to be able to use more of our brains, and share these abilities and powers. I'm not saying it will happen, 'poof', immediately, but I believe it will be the consequence of the change. It is evolution. Evolution explains us as being adaptive based on our environment and promotes survival. Well, the human race needs to adapt. We are destroying the world around us, living only from the mind, acting on impulse instead of using intuition. If this continues, life will not. Life will always find a way to go on. I have enjoyed recently (call me sad) my pet sea-monkeys, little shrimp hatched from eggs from a packet, added to water, and hatch. I think this is a little miracle, how life can be preserved and prevail, beyond all doubt.

So where has all this come from? Well, I have always been fascinated with water. Even as a little girl, I used to love to sit by rock pools and catch fish to study. I have an attraction to streams, lakes, rivers, the sea. I love to be near water. The spiritual symbolism of the element water is stand-out to those who study it, but in case you don't know, it is intuition. It is wisdom, metamorphosis, transformation, subconscious, purification, life and much more. But in this context, I believe my body and my mind, my soul - and other people have been speaking to me and pointing me in the right direction for such a long time. Looking back on it now, it seems obvious to me where I should have been headed. But I'm here now. I have great intuition, and I must use it.

Along with my fascination with water, I have always had dreams of water, primarily of fish. In my dreams, for years, nearly all my life, I have dreamed of having a beautiful pond, or an aquarium of fish. Sometimes in my dreams, I just observe them. But more often than not the climax of my dream is that something happens to the fish: they are thrown out the tank, the water boils, they are injured, they are poisoned. It is quite distressing when I dream it, causes a lot of anxiety. When I started having these dreams, I naturally assumed the worst, and thought they must represent loved ones or friends being injured or dying, or even me facing this fate.

A typical definition of fish from dream dictionaries is that of emotions and feelings, wealth and power. To dream of dead fish represents a fall, perhaps related to these things. Well, if the dreams have only been referring to my life, you will know that I am no stranger to that. I have had my fair share of falls. In fact being bipolar has meant I've seen many rises and falls. However - back to the dream definition - it can also mean spiritual growth or transformation. That, I have certainly undergone.

But, in context of my vision, I believe that this is symbolizing the end of the Age of Pisces. I believe at the moment, we are living in the Age of Pisces. In astrology, the Age of Aquarius follows the Age of Pisces. I did some research and I came across this on a useful site:

"The Dreams: People have been having many water type dreams. Usually they are very scary. Many people are afraid that these dreams are prophetic and that the ocean is going to come over the land and kill everyone. However, other dreams like this portray similar ocean dreams but the dreamer just stands there and watches in awe and feels no fear. Other dreams are about fish tanks which are broken and fish are flopping on the floor helplessly, and others where the tank breaks and water falls to the floor, but the fish swim in the air just like they were still in the water. We have come to think of these dreams, as being prophetic, Yes! However, not that the physical world will be destroyed but that we are undergoing a spiritual change, and these dreams are messages that the Age of Pisces (a water sign) is ending, and that the Age of Aquarius (the water bearer sign) is coming in."

Things started getting exciting for me. A lot of things were making sense. I had written a poem, the poem '2012' a while ago. At the time, this is what I imagined the 2012 transition to be. It seemed clear to me. The words just flowed out of me as if they came from somewhere else. It seemed natural. At the time I passed it off as my overactive imagination. Now, insight has led me to believe I can see into the future. This is what I see. No finality: a new beginning, the Age of Aquarius, the realm of the dolphin, the era of the water bearer.

My message is: do not fear, or live in hate. Live in love, and send positive vibes to everyone, as this will be reflected back to you through the energy transitions of the world. If you are a spiritual person, you know this. If you are not, I recommend you start thinking about it.

THE PROPHECY OF POETRY

Have you ever considered at all that ideas you come up with, things that 'pop' into your head, are messages? It is now my firm belief that a lot of the things you dream up, especially if you are a creative person, can often be a spiritual influence. Some people openly use spirituality as their influence. Think about writers who wrote things way ahead of their generation; some of them are remarkably prophetic. This is especially true with a lot of early science fiction novels, which predicted technological advances that were unaccountably accurate.

George Orwell's novel '1984' is celebrated for its ground-breaking glimpse into a future dystopia in which the elusive Big Brother government monitors on an extreme level. For its day, this idea was massively unrealistic. Yet, in its unrealistic nature was prediction, as we are aware (and if you are unaware, you are blissfully ignorant) that we are monitored so closely now, that the establishment have our records on tap. Facebook and the age of the social network mean that all of our details, our beliefs and backgrounds, our location, and who we know and associate with are handed on a plate to people trying to control us. We all happily update everything about ourselves. Don't get me wrong, I'm not spreading a mass message to close your Facebook account; I myself have a Facebook account. However, it would be blind not to acknowledge that the eye of 'Big Brother' is fixed upon us. In his writing, George Orwell created a prophecy that was accurate: everything right down to it being hidden behind a seemingly reassuring context. Plus, if the world we live in now, with all its tragedy, is not a dystopia then I do not know what is. The prospect can only get more terrifying, more in line with the book.

However, I am not here to spread messages of fear among people. It is fear that is the biggest method of control and keeps us inside the barriers we need to break free from. The future is a Golden Age, one of great enlightenment and allowing the mind to be freed. Our vibrations shall increase, and therefore the vibrations we receive will increase, and with these vibrations comes the knowledge of things that we have never understood, and fear is part of what is stopping us understand.

Looking back on the poetry I wrote, some that was started years ago, it tracks the bitterness, fear and pain, as well as the periods of exhilaration and love, that accompanied my journey to understanding. A lot of it is emotional, a lot of it is tongue in cheek, some is just tribute; but I have only recently realized that throughout my work there are messages. These messages I believe are about the world, and about my own journey. Now, I have always been interested in spiritualism, as I explained, but for many years I have been living from the mind and ego. I have been involved in the gratification and absence of love in myself, and did not feel that I had any spiritual ability, or indeed even really consider the consequences of my actions. Therefore, I have been blind to the effect I had on the world and on myself. I did not fear God; I felt that I was owed something from the world and the fact it was not paying up meant I did not owe anything myself. I did believe in an external force on some level, but what I did not realize is that the greatest power of change is not controlling us completely: the power of God and bending fate are abilities we possess ourselves and are within. This is not to say we are alone and that we do not have destinies. But we have free will, and we must change to fulfil ourselves as people, as souls. This era has been an age lacking in the fear of 'God'. When I say God, I do not speak of a particular religion or endorse that religious teachings are the complete way forward; they are created and interpreted with all the selfish bias of man throughout history. But one thing the belief in higher powers and forces has for those who truly possess it is faith. The faith to think positively, the faith not to fear, and the faith in our own effect upon the universe.

One of my favourite pieces of work, my defining poem, is 'From the Ashes, I will Rise' where I metaphorically likened myself to a Phoenix. This, I believed at the time, was my artistic reflection of Bipolar disorder, and a description of my life to date. I was suffering depressive and manic episodes, highs and lows, falls and so-called 'rises' and I enjoyed thinking of myself as something better than just a mental illness, as a Phoenix. However, looking back, these 'rises' that I had believed in, were not proper rises. Episodes of mania in Bipolar, with everything sped up, meant that I had false glimpses of spiritual reckoning, of energy, of productivity, of love. I felt empowered when the 'mania' hit me, often like I had literally been hit with lightening, but dived into the wrong paths, was led into the arms of wrong people, acted in a way that was still not me. I felt ecstasy, but not true ecstasy, for each road I followed during these episodes was destruction. It felt like many rises and falls, but it wasn't. I was, for many years in a state of suspension, of chrysalis. I was not truly living, I did not have control over the things that I did, and this is why it often led to hurting people and myself. This is not a true rise. I believe that I have now experienced the 'rise' that climaxed my poem, the true awakening that I had spoke of. For how could I have truly seen myself as a powerful creature if I felt I had no control of when and how I 'burst into flames'. The poem was recurrent with the themes of my past, and indicated that I was bound to it. (Could I just step in here and say that all of this was on a subconscious level. As I said, I wrote the metaphor of Bipolar Disorder as a Phoenix with creative writing but no deep analysis). Recovering from mental illness, my 'awakening' has been the true rise from the ashes. The desire to protect and help myself and others, instead of destroy myself and others is the true prophecy I believe behind this poem, the one I have experienced. No, I'm not saying that I will not suffer with depression, or even manic spells in the future, no matter how 'cured' I feel, the fact of the matter is, that a lot of the illness has a biochemical background, and as much as I endorse spirituality it would be counterproductive not to recognize science, for the two come hand in hand. It was the gaining of 'faith' that had meant that I rose from the ashes of illness, the recognition of my own effect on myself and others and my desire to control this in a positive way.

Another poem that was a 'message' to me was that of 'Life Science', where I used a scientific lexis to describe the nature of our existence, as vibrations and electro-magnetic signals that can alter our reality. It is only now I truly recognize the meaning of these words. They are true, we are vibrations, and the everything has an energy, and we can create positive or negative signals to the Universe that communicate back to us. At the time, I wrote this poem with no true faith in the words. They were simply in my eyes, poetic pondering, but without true belief in what I was saying. For how could I have truly, in the midst of the ashes that bound me, say such things and then not carry them out. I always tried to be a good person, even at my worst I liked helping people, but to me, this just meant giving them things. I gave away some very sacred and expensive possessions, simply as acts of so called 'love', and there was an element of love behind them, I did care for these people but I did not really know what it meant to care for anyone, because I did not care for myself. This would lead to a lot of anger, feelings of rejection and disappointment that meant that I undid the present behind these 'gifts' by showing rage and hatred to people when they did not fulfil my self-gratifying needs. If they didn't show me they loved me, I counted them as traitors, as enemies, my past having been so riddled by these. I believe the seemingly worthless incantation of these words in my poem was my higher self whispering direction of what to truly believe in. For the realization of messages that have been there for you from the very beginning is all part of spiritual awakening.

There is way more to comment on, and in the future I will. However I will finish this by discussing drugs, and addiction to them. Drugs I believe, can be the carrier of spiritual forces, however not always positive ones. I believe that to take drugs offers us false glimpses of spiritual states, and elicits how we must subconsciously strive for them. Cannabis, an anxiolytic creates a temporary state of meditation, allowing complete relaxation and spiritual imagery and analyses to take place. Hallucinatory drugs, such as ketamine or acid, allow complete breakdown of the walls of perception, perhaps allowing stronger glimpses into the drug takers 'great unknown' than any other drug. Uppers, such as speed, cocaine, ecstasy or my personal old favourite, mephedrone, allow feelings of higher knowledge, apparent love and empathy for everyone around you, and the universe. However, I am not endorsing taking drugs, I am definitely not saying you should do them - the opposite. They allow spiritual connection but are truly the worst form of gaining access to enlightenment, for they carry paths to darkness, and offer lies mixed in these connections, and promote fear in this fear controlled world. For a drug taker, and for my past self, this meant a lot of things. Fear and paranoia of myself and other people, actual fear from the situations you put yourself in and the people you become involved with, and fear of returning to reality, meaning you chase the drugs.

For the many years I took mephedrone also meant a lot of things. It meant that I was blanketed from reality, to the real beauty of enlightenment that I could feel not being on them, it fed my mental illness, with drug seeking behaviour being the key to prolonging my manic episodes and making them worse, emphasizing the psychosis that accompanies both the episode and the drugs. But for me, I always made excuses for it, because it brought me to something that was truly the most amazing thing I'd felt. Along with these feelings of empathy and love, and in completely temporary self belief, I was able to read people in a completely unpredictable way. People I just met I connected to, and knew everything about their past, was able to pin point issues that mattered to them, and their hopes and desires. Sometimes I even made predictions about people's futures, which came to me in glimpses as I spoke to them. A lot of these have come true, which meant a lot of people actually jestingly called me a psychic. I now believe that it did help me open up my psychic channels, it did let my third eye peep into the world. However, it opens up the channels in the wrong way, in a negative way, and therefore can be the carrier of many negative things, and or people. I often felt during my psychoses that I was possessed, and perhaps this was just the psychoses. But if life means that science and spirituality come hand in hand than perhaps psychoses and spirituality does. I believe in these mentally ill, drug-fuelled states I was the conductor for bad forces and energies, and therefore would give these energies out. It was not nature, it was not natural, the exhilaration of tapping into these forces was short lived and false as it was not done in the true and good way of doing so, so other things 'got let in'. In the poem 'The Drone' I make a prediction about the anti-

Christ, thinking more about the end of the world in 2012, and the book of revelations. The poem is like my higher self and the 'ashen' self arguing. I start off describing mephedrone for all its evils, but contradicting myself saying 'the anti-Christ ain't all bad if you can handle what you've had'. I even begin with, 'You can't have a God without the devil', saying that evil must be present in our lives. Perhaps some of this is true, perhaps I needed to lead an evil life to truly have come to this reckoning, it was all part of my personal journey, however the real message of this poem was predicting my fall, the last greatest one, and it all had been handed to me by mephedrone. I had taken it for years and like I said, fed my illness and led me to evil people, and let to the eventual losing everything, my career, my friends, my mind completely and my last series of attempted overdoses.

A lot of people will read this and attribute my mental illness to the actual taking of drugs. I can assure you this is not the case. It was mental illness through negative events and thoughts that dragged me down to the level of drugs and escapism, and long after I was 'removed' from this life by my family and on prescription drugs, I still suffered all the psychoses of the conditions. I needed to discover 'faith', as I keep saying; the faith that I lacked in myself, the world and of spirituality to truly recover from mental illness and drugs. I can now say, hand on heart I have been clean for a long time, and I am not even tempted to go back down that route. It was not an egotistical decision... (to stop taking drugs) ... not like I quit because I knew it was wrong or bad for me, I just realized that it did not serve my soul or the world for the first time, and it no longer appealed. This is quite something for a former addict, and a sufferer of mental illness to say, let me tell you. To truly accept one's reality as what I want is a massive decision for me. So I believe that in my poem 'The Drone', something or someone was telling me something. I had written 'when you hear it calling, that growling, hissing drone, remember when you are falling that you will never be alone'. Something was telling me to remember that I am not a single entity to the world, the world is connected and we are never alone.

THE STIGMA ATTACHED TO BEING SPIRITUAL

Just wanted to go back to my mental illness here. I had been diagnosed with depression, Bulimia nervosa, and then the following diagnoses of Bipolar type 1, Borderline Personality Disorder and Post-traumatic Stress Disorder. Wow, there's a lot of names for me, when I think about it. A lot of labels for me to believe in and to subconsciously follow. I'm not saying I am none of these things now; I do think that there is a lot of scientific evidence for them in terms of studies and findings and correlations. I think my studies of Psychology helped indoctrinate the importance of experimental research in myself, so therefore I started to believe in my need for psychiatric methods of therapy, i.e. prescription drugs in my case, having read all the appropriate articles.

Now please, please don't think that I am saying that these disorders do not exist or that I never had them. Depression is a terrible illness that can dawn for no apparent reason or external factors. Eating disorders can completely take control over your life, become your life, with your whole world surrounded by your eating and weight. A sufferer of an eating disorder knows this. There's not a moment that it drops from your consciousness. When I started having periods of massive highs and lows, notably rather like taking drugs but without being on drugs, it seemed that my early drug debacles with ecstasy as a young teenager had damaged me. Well, this is what I believed. I was a keen and interested psychology student, and my past drug-taking behaviour, past bulimia, and perhaps possible genetic predisposition made it clear to me, my family and the doctors I was Bipolar type 1. Then after a series of extremely negative events in my life, consequent erratic relationships with people and my floods of emotion and anger associated with my PTSD, it seemed fitting to the doctors that I was Borderline Personality Disorder. It all seemed to fit into place. Why I couldn't maintain relationships and friendships, why I was so angry and upset at the world. Now I am not here to slag off doctors. I massively respect doctors and psychiatrists, they are people trying to help people and working in the mental health industry is no piece of cake, I speak from experience. However to me, looking back, it seems clear to me why my mental health took such massive declines. Whatever you put your energy or emotions towards in life becomes your reality. If you put your energy and emotion into a negative existence, it becomes reality.

Around the time I was diagnosed depression at age 14, is when I left the path of spirituality behind, of empowerment of myself. I looked back at my early beliefs and interests in spirituality and even my practices of Wicca etc as childhood naivety. I had dropped it in a second just to be part of the social group that I had prayed for, and by the time I began my studies as a psychology student, they were long gone. I believed in psychics and mediums at this point, but I no longer believed in the spiritual power of myself, and my spiritual power as an entity of nature and Mother Earth. To be honest, even this was a sign to me. I was dedicated to psychology and to becoming a psychologist; however, I still sort out psychics and mediums. Everything psychology teaches goes against psychics and mediums. They are passed off as con artists and swindlers, and their techniques scrutinized and torn to shreds. Well, in fairness, like everything each socio-economic, cultural, religious or political groups there are people that let others down. It is important to acknowledge that. I believe my soul was telling me to head back towards the route of spirituality because I was always fascinated with clairvoyants etc. However, psychology was telling me it was bullshit. A typical conflict of head over heart.

Let me tell you something in terms of spirituality as a science, in case you are not following what this hippy fruit-loop is saying. The body gives off electro-magnetic signals that are measurable by scientific methods. There has been findings of a great deal on energy coming from the heart, and about the heart's role as a strong communicator to the brain, and the heart has been named as key player in 'perception, cognition and emotional processing'. Interesting as well is the finding that sustained feelings of love synchronize heart rhythms with that of the respiratory and oscillatory systems as well as brain activity. In spirituality there are seven chakras. The heart chakra is named as being key for love, understanding, trust, hope, openness, compassion, balance, forgiveness. Hey, look, I just listed all the key things important to understanding and dealing with people who suffer from any sort of melancholy or negative experience whatsoever. This are, certainly, the final key aspects that helped in my recovery. But back to the original point: my heart was telling me to go towards a spiritual route, I have love and openness for spirituality however my ego and mind were telling me it was stupid and to be a psychologist. So if the heart can, in both spirituality and science, be the key to love and well-being, surely we must follow it? The heart is a master aside the brain in the body, and therefore this represents that love is the decider of our overall well being. You must do what you love, not what is sensible, to increase your well being. I think science would agree with me at least on the well being front. We all in our lives seek love and seek meaning. Maybe it is appropriate to find these by thinking back to the very core basics of what you love. Listen to your heart not your head (most of the time!)

As a psychology student, a mental health patient, and anyone who is aware of the society that we live in, I think it's fair to say that spirituality and its various therapeutic methods have a massive stigma attached to them. In fact one of the interesting things I learnt through being a sufferer and researcher of Bipolar Disorder led me to ask myself and others questions about spirituality. I felt, as a Bipolar, that during my periods of mania that I had spiritual recognition and empowerment. I mentioned before that my periods of taking drugs I also felt this. That was what mania was for me, it was the feeling of being on drugs when not being on drugs, like I never stopped having the high and come down cycle of ecstasy. When I was depressed, I felt like I was in the company or sometimes ruled by bad spirits, and I often felt possessed and unattached from myself. Now these are atypical symptoms of Bipolar and the associated psychoses. However they are, are they not, spiritual beliefs and concepts? Then why, in my medical psychiatric records has it specifically noted these down as being psychoses when they are beliefs. Again, I'd like to reiterate here that I'm not saying either are the spot on answer. You are not definitely possessed or empowered and you are not definitely suffering from a simple brain psychosis and not the subject of spiritual awakening. It is ridiculous on both fronts to rule out one or the other! Nobody in life can say at this moment that they know everything there is to know about the world; therefore it is ignorant not to acknowledge anything. However, the only thing certain here is belief, or faith. As a person, I felt spiritual imbalance in my life, and I believed these things about myself, but I couldn't put my HEART into it because it was more rational to have faith in the medical diagnoses of psychosis and therefore place me as being a victim of an illness rather than a powerful spiritual entity, and one capable of changing the future.

Now this society, your doctor, your family, your friends or even YOU might have stigma against the latter option. Can I just say that, should you not believe it and if someone else believes it, then if you can't say anything nice, don't say nothin' at all? People have the human right and freedom in this society to believe in whatever they want, and it is not for anybody to criticize. The powerful effect of words and response from others is most life-changing, I think everybody can agree to that in both science and spiritualism. If you get called fat at school, when you are older you might have an eating disorder. I have firsthand experience with this. The external social responses of both positive and negative feedback can shape us accordingly, and it takes a very strong person not to come against this unprepared. If you are hurting because of what some idiot said to you then don't worry, you are definitely not alone, and no, we can't always account for negative energy that is being sent to you, to your heart. But, again, the theme here remains constant and you must believe in your cause, and have faith in that these people cannot take it away from you. You are a powerful person, and you can protect yourself emotionally and spiritually as long as you keep this strong faith to your cause and belief in yourself. I am suggesting that the power to heal yourself comes in the belief and faith that things can change, that you can have a happy future rather than anything else.

THE PERSONAL PROPHECY

So, here is what I want to propose. In spirituality, it is said that everything that you put your emotion and energy towards become your reality. This is in terms of the energies that we possess and can transmit as entities within and part of the Universe. When you truly believe in this, as I do, then you think more about the effect you have on the Universe. For example, when you are happy it can make other people happy; when you laugh you can make other people laugh; when you are unhappy it can definitely make other people unhappy; and this is the same with anger. In spirituality we have vibrations and these vibrations are what help to shape our existence. If you put positivity in the world, you get positivity back. There is a lot of variation on this, for example, Karma in Indian religions, the Pagan concept of the what you send out coming back threefold and Dharma, the Buddhist concept of upholding the natural order of things in the Universe. If you want to create a loving harmonious world, then you must be loving and harmonious. It's all about cause and effect really, if you give out good you get good back, same way if you give out bad you get bad back. I think these concepts, ones that I have always acknowledged but not always embraced are very important, and I have been able to apply them to my own experience of mental health and life.

Thing is, it's so easy to be negative when you are unhappy or depressed. I'm sure quite a few of us can say that we have projected a negative attitude on to the world when we have been having a bad time. In particular for me, mine was anger... I was angry at my past, angry at myself, and angry at the world. In the end, it only really made people angry with me. People tried to be understanding as they could with me, but you can't bank on the tenacity of others. If people show you anger or depression back then it lets you down further, because all we are really looking for is love, understanding, trust and compassion. It is the same concept of positive thinking to change your future, for example the cognitive triad in psychology emphasizing a need to change thoughts about the self, the world and the future. The difference is that this carries a belief that these thoughts have vibrations that can actually change the atmosphere and alter your own universe. Yes, life will always chuck things at you that we can't account for. Some of these will contain serious heartbreak and knockbacks: that's just life. But if we tell ourselves we are gonna be strong, and things will change for the better, then we are sending that positive vibration to the universe, and lo and behold we are gifted with the powers of strength and the power to make things better, and deal with things.

So what do I think has helped my recovering? I like to write poetry and be creative and I tracked my own journey with creative writing. But I also explained my belief in that I was sent messages from higher forces and the other side when actively doing the writing, and I was able to hide clues for myself in the poetry that would eventually lead me to the right path and lead me to who I really was in the midst of an illness. My belief in this is very spiritual, but I do not want to impose my beliefs on anybody. Your belief is your own, it must be in order to work. (I always believed in spirituality and forced to believe psychology). You can look at different perspectives of this. You can look at it from the subconscious, that I delivered myself positive thoughts about my future that were delivered through my creative writing. You can look at it from environmental factors to. As soon as I started writing messages of a happier future that I must have projected that image and people responded to it and this was gratifying. Either way, somewhere in there, in all the depression and psychosis was faith in myself, and belief. I simply needed to realize it.

I propose that you start writing, painting, singing, writing a diary or doing anything that inspires you creatively. If you are not a creative person, then keep records of your thoughts, ideas and influences. You need to open up these creative channels and let them explode out of you. A lot of us will be feeling very negative and low, and this is OK to talk about, to express. So, if it begins with artistic work reflecting your negativity, then start with that. You need to turn this creative medium into a reflection of you so therefore let it be accurate, and really let all of the emotions and pent up feelings be shared onto these creative works.

But these negative thoughts and feelings cannot go on forever, and you want them to change. I propose you make a prophecy about yourself. You do not have to believe in divination or spirituality but you must let the ideas come to you. If you don't want to see it as a prophecy, see it as being optimistic, because more importantly it has to be POSITIVE. So if you are letting your creative juices flow and all you are getting is negative images, ideas and thoughts you must literally chuck them out. Laugh at them, scoff at them, because this person you are transforming to only looks at things in a good and happy way, in a hope they can have a good and happy effect on the world. If nothing positive comes to you naturally, then think about what you wish would happen to you. What you wish, but don't at the moment believe is possible. Try and transform the opening "I wish there was" to "there will be" and let this link to the creative flair that you have started to develop. Let the muse burst alive and help you to express it and this positive prophecy. For me, it was a Phoenix, rising from the ashes, coming back from the dead despite all doubt, and transforming. You can use metaphors for your prophecy such as this, or anything that is personal or interesting to you.

You must build up this work, and at the start you may have been portraying mixed messages, both pessimistic and optimistic. This is fine, however, make sure that you start to let the optimistic overcome the pessimistic. Even if you don't consciously agree with them, let optimistic ideas win over the negative ones at least in your creativity or work if not in your conscious mind. Let it spill out of you. If you are stuck for ideas, look back at joys of your past, things that interest you (try not to let them be morbid) and things that make you laugh. Music is also a very powerful tool, listen to music, preferably ones that inspire happy or calming emotions, and work to them. Try not to let all the wishes and hopes be too self-centred, or self-gratifying. Try and extend them. For example, "I want to be happy" becomes "I want to be happy so that I can make other people happy, too" and continue with these concepts until you are creating work and leaving these messages for yourself without consciously doing so.

The rest of it requires a little magic. (I'm not saying literal magic, or am I?) You need to believe in these messages of optimism. If you are a pessimist, then slap yourself out of it! You are a good person, there is no reason that these ideas for the future cannot happen for you. Why can't they? There is no good real reason, so stop making excuses for yourself! They will happen! If you can't change your inner emotions and thoughts straight away, then actively change your outer ones and make them show. Be nice to people. Be kind, be understanding, be loving. Be everything that you want for yourself and expect back. Don't respond to anger as much as you can. Tell yourself you are strong, and that you are calm and react like that. You will be most pleased with the rewards. If you act strongly and calmly in an argument, without showing bitterness or hate, you've acted the right way and people will respond to it, even if the response is just the non-continuation of the argument. Have faith in yourself, your work and your prophecy if you can't have immediate faith in other people, for this is all you need.

This is not an overnight process, but work at it! And build on it! You may be happy and surprised with at least what you have been able to produce. But stick at it, and use all your want for it to happen become the energy pushing you to continue, believe in it! You should get a lot of self-expression out, and be able to explore lots of different ideas and outputs. But eventually your prophecy should become clear to you. It is a 'personal' prophecy, so everybody will have their own, but eventually the message should be getting through to you of what your own one is. My own Prophecy was:

"From the Ashes, I will Rise".

WHO ARE YOU?

If you start focussing on the prophecy, I feel sure
that you can fulfil it, just like I did. But along with
working on the prophecy, it is important to give
meaning to your existence, and give yourself worth.
I spoke briefly about how when society puts labels
and categories on us we often embrace them;
furthermore, we often decide that we are
something. Sadly, this more often than not is a
negative association to the self.
Like I said at the beginning, I had been diagnosed
with depression, Bipolar, Bulimia, Borderline
Personality Disorder and Post-traumatic Stress
Disorder, therefore I was these diagnoses. It's like I
applied all my personal characteristics to being part
of these diagnoses, as if there was no individuality
to me, no room for change. I had been bullied in the
past, had a lot of people go against me and was
called fat, ugly, crazy, a druggie, a slut, sometimes
evil. It's like I completely took these on board, with
them becoming my very existence. I felt as though
my own name carried negative connotations. I
hated myself and therefore was not proud of being
who I was.
I invite everybody, not just those who are suffer
with mental health problems, but anybody to truly
name themselves. If you are going to stick with
your original name, then I want you to think about
your achievements. Are you trained in anything?
Have you completed or are working on your
studies? What is your job role? Even if you don't
like your job, have pride in the fact you have one.
Or alternatively, what are you good at it? Do you
like art? Then you are an artist. If you are into films,

then you are a film expert. If you are very sociable then you are a social butterfly. But I also want you to look into yourself even further, and pick out what the good aspects of your personality: are you kind? Caring? Sympathetic? Have you been through a lot? Are you a survivor?

My point is that it is very easily to apply and embrace labels. In a society where everything and everyone is stereotyped, it is almost impossible to avoid. I suggest that we transform ourselves into a positive label, a positive role, a positive entity. Perhaps the word stereotype made you shudder in that sentence? Then you are an individual! You like to embrace your independence and originality.

As a writer I like to use imagery and metaphors, and now I want to apply a positive image to myself, it only felt right after I wrote 'From the Ashes, I WILL RISE' that I am a Phoenix. I rose from the depths of mental illness and showed remarkable strength and recovery. I'm not saying that everybody should apply a mythical creature to themselves, but perhaps find a symbol that you respect and which embodies everything that you love. You can be anything you want.

I became the Indigo Heart when I came to spiritual awareness: it represents me as an Indigo child, one born into a generation of change, highly sensitive, highly aware and able to work with energies. I am a very spiritual person.

If we are proud of who we are and refer to ourselves (even if only in our heads) as an amazing, powerful, wonderful being, then we will start to embody it and send positive vibrations into the world - for we all are such beings; we simply need only realize it.

I am the Indigo heart, the Phoenix, I am the spiritualist, poet, carer, scholar, humanitarian, light worker, and published author! I am Marguerite Leathley Who are you?